It's Time To Be Me

A Practical Guide To Finding And Being
Your Authentic Self

Carolyn G.A Ching

Published by

It's Time To Be Me
A Practical Guide To Finding And Being Your Authentic Self

Carolyn G.A Ching

First Printing: January 2025

Purple Hibiscus Media, Kailua-Kona, Hawaii

Carolyn Ching is available to speak at your business or conference event on a variety of topics. She holds retreats and personal breakthrough sessions on the Big Island of Hawaii and the Sunshine Coast in Australia. Carolyn works with clients from all over the world via Zoom and is also available for in-person sessions.

Contact her at www.absoluteawareness.net or www.absoluteawareness.com.au

Please join our community on Facebook and share your story of transformation.

(Facebook page: It's Time To Be Me)

https://www.facebook.com/share/4bx2vEqwV5A7Uy5h/?mibextid=LQQJ4d

Why Read This Book?

Are you tired of living a life that doesn't feel like your own? Do you constantly find yourself:

– Saying "Yes" when you want to say "No"?
– Sacrificing your dreams to meet others' expectations?
– Feeling like you're just existing, not truly living?

It's time to change!

Through powerful, real-life client stories and practical strategies, Carolyn draws from over two decades of experience helping people just like you reclaim their identity and reignite their inner spark. Whether you've been in a relationship that dimmed your light, or you've spent years trying to fit into everyone else's expectations, this transformative guide will help you:

· Uncover your true passion and purpose in life

· Rebuild your self-worth

· Gain the courage, confidence, and clarity to be authentically you

Written with compassion and understanding, this book is more than a guide—it's a gentle companion on your journey back to yourself. Carolyn's approach is warm, accessible, and tailored to meet you exactly where you are, helping you take powerful steps at your own pace.

Are you ready to stop surviving and start thriving? Your journey to self-discovery begins now.

Take the first step. Open this book. Transform your life.

Written by a leading expert with over twenty years of experience.

Carolyn G.A Ching is the author of *Anxiety The Book*. She is a certified hypnotherapist and member of ICBCH and IICT. Carolyn is also a registered nurse, professional counselor, neuro-linguistic programming practitioner, and a Time Line Therapy® practitioner and trainer. She is a sought-after speaker at conferences in the USA, Australia, and worldwide.

What Others Are Saying About This Book

"*It's Time To Be Me* is a heartfelt guide that explores the deep impact of living out of alignment with your true self. With warmth and wisdom, Carolyn reveals how inauthentic living affects your overall health and well-being. Through practical action steps, she gently leads you on a transformative journey toward embracing your authentic, valuable self. Discover why aligning with your true desires is essential and learn how to implement life-changing strategies that empower you to live fully and authentically."

—Denise Morrison,
Certified Integrative Health
Practitioner/Trauma-Informed Coach

"Through compelling real-life examples and transformative exercises, this book doesn't just tell you to 'be yourself'—it shows you how. This isn't just another self-help book; it's a life-changing companion for the journey to self-discovery."

—Vera Stewart-Lutz,
CHT, Solutions Hypnotherapy, Arizona.

"It's Time to Be Me is a delightful book, full of important information for those wishing to break from the exhausting cycle of people-pleasing and self-doubt. With her warm heart and masterful pen, Carolyn inspires us to dissolve unhealthy "shoulds", and to embrace meaningful self-discovery and sustainable happiness. As a CEO of a nonprofit helping children and adults who are victims of domestic violence, I find Carolyn's latest book to be honest, accessible, and refreshing."

—Carol, Hawaii

Author's Note

I'm so excited that you are embarking on a wonderful journey of change. I would like to thank all the amazing clients I've had the privilege of working with; my editor, Ita de Groot, for helping me make this book a reality; and Richard Nongard for sharing his expertise in writing books. I'd also like to send huge thanks to my son and daughter-in-law for always supporting me and accepting me as I am. This book is dedicated to my gorgeous grandson Bradley; may he always have the courage to be himself!

Table of Contents

Chapter One

What Does Being Authentic Mean?

"Authenticity is the daily practice of letting go of who we think we're supposed to be and embracing who we are."

—Brené Brown

In more than twenty years as a therapist, one of the things I've noticed is just how common it is for people to not know who they truly are or to "wear a mask" or change their personality around others just to fit in or be accepted. It can be likened to a chameleon, changing its colors to blend in with its environment.

Living life in this way can take a toll on your personal health, well-being, relationships, and, of course, life choices.

Take a moment to answer these questions honestly for yourself:

- Do you ever feel like you're living your life to please others?

- Did someone make a judgment about you, and one, five, ten, or more years later you're still altering who you truly are because of that one statement?

- Are you a cat person pretending to be a dog person because all your friends love dogs?

- Do you play down your accomplishments or intelligence around certain people?

- Have you had Botox, tattoos, or cosmetic surgery because that's what your friends do or that's what your partner wants? Or maybe you think changing your appearance will give you confidence?

- Do you have difficulty making choices or decisions because you worry about what other people might think?

- Are you staying in a job that you hate because you think that's what's expected of you or because other people approve of you doing that job?

- Have you lost yourself in a relationship?

- Do you feel as though you're just going through the motions, and nothing makes you genuinely happy?

If you've answered "Yes" to any of these questions, the chances are you are not living your life being your true or authentic self.

Let me share with you the story of a client I had the privilege of working with in Hawaii.

Claire had it all, or at least that's what everyone around her thought. At thirty-five, she was a successful marketing executive and a loving mother to her two children, a boy and a girl. She was the wife of her college sweetheart, David. Her Instagram and Facebook feeds were carefully curated collections of family outings, career achievements, and nights out with friends.

From the outside, her life seemed perfect. But underneath all that, Claire felt like she was drowning.

Every morning, she'd wake up with a sense of dread, forcing herself to go through the motions of her daily routine. At work, she excelled, but her heart wasn't in it. The creativity she'd once loved about marketing had been replaced by spreadsheets and endlessly long, dull, and boring meetings. She found herself envying the enthusiasm and energy that the younger staff members had and wishing she could feel like that.

At home, Claire was the epitome of a supermom, juggling her children's activities, keeping the house clean, and preparing home-cooked meals most nights. However, the constant pressure to meet everyone's needs left her feeling exhausted, empty, and resentful.

Even her friendships felt superficial. Girls' nights out, which had once been a source of fun and joy, now felt like a performance where everyone competed to prove how well they were doing. Claire found herself saying what she thought others wanted to hear instead of expressing her true thoughts and feelings.

Her marriage to David was stable and secure but without passion. They operated more like efficient business partners than loving partners, and most of their conversations had become limited to logistics and child-rearing.

The turning point came on Claire's thirty sixth birthday. As she blew out the candles on her cake, surrounded by family, she realized she couldn't remember the last time she'd made a wish for herself. What did she want? Who was she, really, beneath all the roles she played? And finally, recognizing just how unhappy she was, she booked a session with me.

In our sessions, we discovered that when she was in college, Claire loved to make jewelry and was really good at it. Aware that she should get a "proper" job, she had never pursued it further, and once she started full-time work, she had lacked the time to keep up her old passion.

Claire told me that she decided to look for her old jewelry box, filled with pieces she'd made in college. As she looked through it, memories flooded back: the satisfaction of creating something beautiful and unique with her own hands, the meditative focus of working with delicate materials, and the joy of seeing someone wear her creations. She remembered how good it felt to create special pieces for the people she loved; her mother still wore a necklace Claire had created many years earlier.

In the days that followed, inspired by her memories, Claire found her old tools that were packed away in the garage and ordered some basic supplies online. Claire shared with me that when the package arrived, she felt a flutter of excitement she hadn't experienced in years. Late at night, after the kids were in bed, she began to experiment with wire-wrapping crystals and some semi-precious stones she had.

As the weeks passed, Claire found herself looking forward to her evenings of creativity. The intricate work of manipulating wire around beautiful stones was challenging, requiring complete focus, but was deeply satisfying. She found that as soon as she sat down to create something, her tiredness disappeared. She started learning new techniques from online tutorials and saw her skills improve with each piece she made.

The journey back to being her authentic self wasn't easy. Claire started saying "No" to things that were not congruent with her values rather than saying "Yes" to please others, and in the beginning, she experienced some guilt about prioritizing her own needs. There were a few days when she wondered if it would just be easier to slip back into her old patterns.

The hardest conversation was with David. Years of unspoken frustrations and unmet needs poured out. It was painful but cathartic. They decided to attend couples therapy— committed to rediscovering their connection and improving their communication.

After discovering what her values around her career were, Claire decided she wanted to quit her job so that she could focus on her family and jewelry making. Her old job wasn't in alignment with her values, and she realized this was causing her to feel unhappy and unfulfilled. They agreed they could manage financially if she could find a part-time job.

Once you are living your life authentically, opportunities start showing up, and Claire found part-time work in a local jewelry store. Her new employer even paid for her to do a certification course in gemstones.

Claire began making small changes in other aspects of her life too. She explored assertive communication strategies and, as a result, had some honest conversations with her friends, sharing her rediscovered passion, her decision to quit her job, and her struggles. Some of her friendships deepened, and a few dropped off, making room for new connections with fellow jewelry-making enthusiasts.

By honoring her true self, Claire felt more alive. The empty feeling was gone, and her relationships were becoming more meaningful. Her work, although paying much less than her marketing job, felt more aligned with her creative spirit, and she no longer dreaded going to work. Even at home with her children, she felt more creative, often doing arts and crafts projects with them.

A year after her thirty-sixth birthday, I went to a local craft fair, and there was Claire in a small booth, surrounded by her handmade jewelry. It wasn't a grand boutique or a fancy store, and it was just a small collection of beautifully made, unique pieces, but to Claire it represented so much more. It was a testament to her journey; to the courage it had taken to peel away the layers of old beliefs and expectations and rediscover her true self. Her children were there, excitedly pointing out their favorite pieces to customers, and Claire said to me, "I wish I'd had the courage to do this sooner!"

She wasn't perfect, and her life wasn't without challenges. But for the first time in a long time, Claire felt like she was truly living as herself and expressing her creativity in a way that resonated with her soul. And that made all the difference!

So, what is "being authentic"?

Being authentic is all about being real, about being able to just be yourself, no matter where you are or who you are with. (It's like showing up to a party in your favorite comfortable clothes instead of dressing up to impress.)

When you're authentic, you're not trying to be more sophisticated or smarter than you really are, nor are you diminishing yourself or your achievements. When you are being authentic, you're not trying to be someone else to please others or be accepted by others. In short, you're not trying to be different from who you really are; you're just being you and feeling comfortable with that!

It's not about being perfect! Being authentic doesn't mean you're always happy or that you've got it all figured out. It just means that you're honest about who you are, including the messy parts (and yes, we all have them!). It's like posting a selfie without a filter—you're showing the real you, not some touched-up version.

Living authentically is:

1. Being Honest: Saying what you actually think and feel, even if it's not what others want to hear. But remember, you can be honest and kind at the same time.

2. Showing Your Emotions: If you're sad, you don't pretend to be happy. If you're excited, you don't hide behind a poker face. If you're angry, you don't bottle it up or act passive-aggressively. You allow yourself to acknowledge your true emotions and are not afraid to communicate your feelings with others.

3. Honoring Your Values: You don't change your body or what you believe in just to fit in. If you think something is wrong, you say so or opt out of the activity, even if you're the only one who thinks that way.

4. Admitting Mistakes: When you make a mistake or mess up, you own it. You don't try to blame others or make excuses for your actions. Everyone makes mistakes; it's a natural part of being human, and a mistake is simply feedback that we can do it differently next time.

5. Being Okay with Not Knowing: You're not afraid to say "I don't know" or ask for help when you need it.

6. Following Your Own Path: You make choices and decisions based on what feels right to you rather than what others think you should do.

There are a number of reasons why people fall into the trap of not being themselves; the most common are listed below:

- Fear of not fitting in.

- Pressure to be perfect.

- Old habits.

- Protecting ourselves from getting hurt.

While it can be daunting to explore and change who you truly are and realize what your passion and purpose are, there are many benefits to living an authentic life rather than simply going through the motions of an inauthentic life every day.

The Benefits of Being Authentic

1. Real Friendships: When you're real, you attract people who like you for who you are, and you can have honest and open

conversations even if you don't agree on a topic.

2. Less Stress: You don't have to remember which version of yourself you are to different people or tiptoe around people, hiding parts of yourself.

3. Feeling Better: When you are in alignment with your own values and beliefs, you will notice yourself feeling happier, more joyful, and experiencing more inner peace.

4. Increased Confidence: The more you practice being the true you, the more comfortable you become in your own skin.

5. Better Decisions: When you're true to yourself, it's easier to have clarity and know what you really want in life.

6. Inspiring Others: By being authentic, you inspire other people to be real too.

Being authentic isn't about oversharing or ignoring other people's feelings. You can be real and still be kind and respectful. It's about finding that optimal point where you're true to yourself while still being a good person to others.

Being your authentic self means having the courage to be imperfect, real, and totally yourself. It might feel scary at first, but the more you do it, the more natural it becomes. And the best part? There's only one you in the entire world, and by being authentic, you're letting that unique, awesome person shine through!

By the end of this book, you will have the tools and knowledge to finally be yourself and live a life that is meaningful to you. The good news is that it doesn't matter how old you are when you discover the joy of being yourself; all that matters is that you allow yourself the opportunity to discover YOU!

Chapter Two

The Hidden Cost of Losing Yourself & How to Recalibrate Your COMPASS

*"Don't compromise yourself.
You are all you've got."*

—Janis Joplin

Over the years, I've worked with many clients who have lost sight of themselves in a relationship or are anxious in a job, unhappy and unfulfilled in their marriage, burnt out from always trying to please everyone around them, or feel distanced from their emotions—not able to truly feel happy or excited, content, joyful, etc.

Some of these clients appear to have everything going for them: a great job, beautiful car, awesome partner, great children, travel, material goods, friends, etc. However, there is one common thread that all of them have—they have disconnected from their true self, from their own values and beliefs, in an attempt to live up to perceived expectations of those around them.

Some of these clients even say, "I shouldn't complain," "I have everything, but I just don't feel happy," or "I never feel satisfied. I'm always looking for the next thing to bring me pleasure, even though that pleasure is short-lived."

Other clients book sessions because they don't know what their passion is. The years are ticking by, and they still don't feel as though they have a passion or a purpose in life.

One of my clients, Simon, was in his late forties and had everything he thought he should want: a high-paying corporate job at which he was well respected, a lovely wife, three beautiful kids, and a large house in a nice neighborhood. They had two cars, were able to take skiing trips as a family each year and other vacations as and when they wanted to, and yet he always felt as though something was missing in his life. Simon never really felt fulfilled or happy. Even when he won awards at work, he was always looking for the next thing to give him a sense of achievement, no matter how fleeting.

At home, he often felt resentful and frustrated that he was always fitting in with what Jazmin and the kids wanted to do.

Simon always looked well-groomed and dressed in expensive clothing. He was pleasant to anyone he encountered and was always ready with a smile—a smile that never quite reached his eyes.

Recently, out of the blue, Simon began experiencing regular migraine headaches. He changed his diet and cut down on his drinking (which wasn't heavy to begin with). Simon underwent a range of medical tests that didn't show anything abnormal. His doctor questioned him about stress, but everything seemed fine.

One Thursday, he developed a migraine so strong that he couldn't get out of bed. That morning, after everyone left the house, he lay there feeling miserable. He asked himself how his life had ended up like this, constantly feeling a nagging emptiness inside.

Over the weekend, while he was recovering from the migraine, he started to think seriously about his life. He'd always been a people pleaser, wanting approval, wanting people to like him, respect him, and love him.

When he was in high school, he joined the rugby team because that was what his dad had wanted him to do. Simon loved art and had wanted to join the art classes at school. That wasn't an option for him. After school, he studied business and commerce at university. He was the first member of his family to get a place at university and felt the weight of making his parents proud of him. He never partied or socialized much, as he needed to ensure that he would graduate. He did so with honors.

Several times while he was at university, he wished he could switch to the arts degree but knew that he couldn't bring this up with his parents as they wouldn't see it as a valid career path.

After university, he got a great job in a corporate environment, performed well, and was promoted many times.

He met and married Jazmin. They got on well together; his parents loved her, and everyone said they made the perfect couple, even though Simon wasn't sure that he loved her.

After a year, they had their first son. His parents were happy and excited to be grandparents. Soon one child turned into three. Simon threw himself into work, stayed late, and always said "Yes" to requests from his boss, wanting to make sure his boss liked and valued him and that his position would be secure so he could be a "good provider" for his family.

Thinking about his job, Simon realized that although he was good at it, he actually didn't enjoy it very much—it was just something he knew how to do. When his son started to show signs of being interested in art at school, Simon encouraged it. He found that helping his son with creative projects was one of the only things that genuinely felt good to him.

That weekend, Simon couldn't sleep. He had a restless feeling flowing through his entire body. He lay awake trying to remember the last time he made a decision that was purely for himself, that was based on his own desires rather than what other people expected of him, and came to the sad realization that he couldn't remember a time. He spent most of his life up until this point being the person that everyone else wanted him to be: the good son, good husband, good father, good worker, good colleague, good person, and in the process, had completely lost himself, his true self. He felt as though he had no idea how to get himself out of living a life he didn't want. This is what motivated him to take the first step to getting himself back, by picking up his phone and booking a session with me.

If you are going through your life not being your true self, you are probably experiencing some of the following:

1. Emotional distress

Constantly pretending to be someone that you're not or suppressing your true feelings can lead to anxiety, depression, and a general sense of unease. The anxiety comes from constantly monitoring what you are doing or saying to fit in with other people's perceived expectations. Depression can arise from not feeling fulfilled in life and therefore feeling as though there is no purpose. Often people begin to experience frustration and resentment toward others and themselves because they are spending the majority of their time doing things they don't really want to do and gain little or no pleasure from. When all of this continues over a long period, you are likely to experience a general feeling of unease, unhappiness, and dissatisfaction with life.

2. Loss of self

Over time, living inauthentically can cause you to lose touch with your true self, your values, your worth, and your desires. Eventually, you may even have difficulty knowing what your own preferences, desires, values, and beliefs are and experience confusion about your purpose in life or the goals in your life and what truly matters to you as a person. There can be a sense of disconnection from your emotions and also from your intuition. In relationships, you may adopt your partner's opinions, values, likes, and dislikes without even questioning them.

3. Shallow relationships

When you're not being authentic or if you don't even know who you are, it's challenging to form deep and meaningful connections with other people, and as a result of this, relationships and friendships might feel superficial and not fulfilling. You may find yourself unable to be vulnerable and open with others for fear that they don't like/won't accept who you truly are. Frequently, romantic relationships end in disappointment because you're attracting the relationship based on false pretenses, and who the other person sees is, not who you truly are. One of the dangers in relationships is that at the beginning of a relationship, you may go along with doing all the things the other person enjoys, e.g. going to a horror movie when you hate that type of movie, going to a sporting event when you dislike sport, going to a restaurant when you already know that you dislike that type of food, or pretending to like dogs because your prospective partner has two. When you do all these things without communicating your likes and dislikes, the new partner thinks that this is who you truly are! You might be able to keep up the facade for six months or more before the resentment that has been building up starts to cause cracks in the relationship.

4. Decreased self-esteem

Living up to other people's expectations rather than your own can eat away at self-worth and confidence. Things that you achieve have little or no meaning because they're not aligned with your true desires. There may be a constant sense that you're not measuring up to an impossible standard or are not good enough. It's common to find yourself struggling with self-acceptance and self-love and in many cases, your sense of self-worth becomes dependent on validation from other people. For example, constantly needing recognition in a relationship that your partner loves you, wants you, won't leave you, finds you attractive, etc., or needing the approval and recognition of the boss at work, or seeking the approval of a parent—always trying to live up to what you think their expectation of you is. Some people find themselves constantly seeking validation from friends regarding decisions rather than being happy with their own decisions.

5. Missed opportunities

By not pursuing your true passions or expressing your genuine thoughts and ideas, you will miss out on both personal and professional growth opportunities. Often, you won't even notice opportunities that could be more satisfying and fulfilling. As a result of not being true to what's important to you, chances to develop your unique talents and skills are missed. You fail to recognize opportunities that are aligned with your true self and will find yourself avoiding taking risks that might lead to personal growth, instead settling for a life that's safe and unfulfilling.

6. Increased stress

Maintaining the fake you requires constant effort and monitoring, which can be mentally and emotionally draining. You go through life constantly being on guard, monitoring what you say and what you do, or feeling anxious about slipping up. Making a simple decision becomes difficult and stressful, and you may find yourself needing to get validation from others that the decision you're making is the right one. Eventually, physical symptoms like headaches, irritable, bowel syndrome, insomnia or chronic fatigue syndrome may occur.

7. Lack of fulfillment

There can be a sense of emptiness or dissatisfaction in life from achieving goals or acquiring possessions that don't align with your authentic self; things can become meaningless, and you might feel a sense of emptiness, even after reaching major milestones or accomplishments. For many people, this plays out with them constantly seeking the next achievement or the next thing that will bring them happiness, even though that happiness is short-lived. When you're living an unfulfilled life, it can feel like you're simply going through the motions every day on autopilot, and there may be a constant nagging sense that something is missing from your life, even if you don't really know what it is that's missing.

8. Regret

Frequently, later in life, people find that they regret having lived their life for other people rather than pursuing their own passions. Sometimes, people feel they wasted part of their lifetime and are mourning lost opportunities or things they gave up in order to be with someone or for taking on a career they weren't passionate about. All this regret can cause a midlife or late-life crisis, and for some it becomes difficult to find peace and contentment in later life.

9. Difficulty in decision-making

When you are disconnected from your true self, making important life decisions becomes challenging and can lead to choices that you regret. Sometimes this is in the form of body art such as tattoos, cosmetic surgery, career choices, financial choices, health, housing, or partner choices. The common theme when you're disconnected from your true self is not being able to trust your own judgment, second-guessing the choices that you make, and allowing decisions to be influenced by other people's opinions. There is also a tendency to make decisions based on what you think you should do rather than what you actually want to do. Some people find themselves paralyzed (analysis paralysis) when faced with important life choices, not being able to think clearly, not being able to make a decision, not knowing what is right for them. One of my clients, a single lady in her sixties, was looking to buy a house for her retirement years. She found an affordable house in a nice neighborhood, and the layout was exactly what she wanted and had earlier even drawn from her imagination on paper, but after talking it over with a family member who didn't like the location, my client discounted it and ended up buying a property that needed work done to it and had a much larger yard than she could handle. She was miserable living there and slid into depression.

10. Impaired creativity

Being your authentic self fuels creativity, and so when people behave in a way that is not in alignment with their true selves, natural creative impulses are stifled, leading to creative blocks or a sense of being stuck. This makes it difficult to be able to think outside the box or come up with original ideas, and the joy and fulfillment that come from expressing creativity is diminished or lost completely.

Emma, aged twenty-eight, had always been self-conscious about her nose. Since her teenage years, she had been convinced it was the root of all her insecurities. After years of saving, she finally took the plunge and scheduled a rhinoplasty. The weeks leading up to the surgery were filled with excitement and anticipation. Emma pored over before-and-after photos, imagining how her life would change once she had the perfect nose. She daydreamed about newfound confidence, better job prospects, and maybe even finding love.

The surgery went well, and Emma got through the recovery phase, focusing on the end result. When the bandages finally came off, she stared at her reflection, heart pounding. Her new nose was exactly what she'd asked for—straight, refined, and beautiful. Emma was elated! She constantly took selfies, loving her new appearance. Friends and family complimented her, and she felt a surge of confidence she'd never experienced before. She even found the courage to ask out a coworker she'd been admiring for a while.

But as weeks turned into months, a familiar unease began to creep back in. Despite her new nose, Emma still found herself hesitating to speak up in meetings. She still felt awkward at parties, not wanting to socialize. Her date with the coworker had been fine, but she spent the entire evening worrying about what he thought of her, barely able to enjoy herself, and then continually analyzing things he had said in the days after the date.

One weekend, as she was getting ready for a friend's wedding, Emma looked at herself in the mirror. She realized that even though her nose was perfect, her negative inner dialogue hadn't disappeared. Instead of her nose, she was now finding fault with her hips, her thighs, and her hair. With a sinking feeling, Emma realized that changing her appearance hadn't magically transformed her self-esteem.

At the wedding, Emma hid in the bathroom, fighting back tears. One of the bridesmaids, noticing her distress, gently asked what was wrong, and Emma found herself sharing that she had thought fixing her nose would fix everything, but she still didn't feel confident or good enough. The bridesmaid listened and then shared her own struggles with self-esteem, telling Emma that it took her years to realize that confidence comes from within, not from external enhancements.

Their conversation was a wake-up call for Emma. She realized that while there was nothing wrong with wanting to change her appearance, she'd been hoping the surgery would solve deeper issues—issues that required inner work, not a scalpel. The bridesmaid gave her my card...

COMPASS

This acronym consists of seven factors that can lead us astray from our authentic path and reminds us that these challenges are like a faulty compass, leading us away from our true north. By recognizing and addressing these issues, we can recalibrate our internal compass and navigate toward a more authentic and fulfilling life journey.

Comparison to others

Living in the shadow of others' achievements can dim your own light. We often measure our worth against an idealized version of someone else's life, forgetting that everyone's journey is unique. Remember that those Instagram and Facebook posts are just a snapshot of someone—not their life 24/7. Constant comparison robs us of happiness in our own progress and blinds us to our strengths.

Overthinking

The paralysis of analysis can trap us in a cycle of inaction. We become so caught up in exploring every possible scenario, spending so much time delving into various tangents that we miss opportunities to act authentically. We may find ourselves overthinking every comment someone has made, rehashing whole conversations, and dwelling on anything we perceive as negative or hurtful, blowing it out of proportion, and ultimately feeling bad about something they actually didn't say! Allowing all these thoughts to run like a hamster on a wheel is exhausting and prevents us from trusting our instincts and expressing ourselves.

Misaligned values

When we live according to other people's expectations (perceived or real) or societal norms that don't resonate with us, rather than living by what is important and meaningful to us, we lose touch with our true selves. This misalignment creates internal conflict and can lead to feelings of emptiness or dissatisfaction, even when we achieve external "success."

People pleasing

The constant need for approval can lead us to shape-shift into who we think others want us to be, like a chameleon changing its colors to fit in with the background. Saying "Yes" to things that are not right for you and always putting someone else's needs before your own not only drains your energy but also erodes your sense of self over time.

Avoidance of discomfort

Personal growth often requires stepping out of our comfort zone, but fear of discomfort can keep us stagnant. Perhaps we are too scared to express our opinion because it's different from someone else's. Maybe we stay in a job we hate because we don't want our parents to be disappointed in us. By avoiding challenges or difficult emotions, we miss out on opportunities to grow as a person or express our true nature, and we miss out on being able to experience the peace and happiness that comes from accepting yourself.

Self-doubt

The negative inner voice or inner critic can be a powerful force undermining our confidence and convincing us we're not good enough or worthy enough. This persistent self-doubt can prevent us from pursuing our dreams, following our purpose, or expressing our true selves, keeping us trapped in a limited version of who we could be.

Social conditioning

From an early age, we're shaped by our environment, culture, and upbringing, often internalizing ideas about how we "should" live, think, behave, or look. This social programming can create a disconnect between our true selves and the persona we present to the world. Breaking free from deeply ingrained social conditioning requires conscious effort and courage to question and subsequently change the limiting beliefs that are holding us back. It's about recognizing which parts of our identity are genuinely ours and which are merely a result of our social environment, for example, doing or accepting certain things because they're part of the workplace culture or your peer group, or altering your appearance so that it fits society's expectations of what beautiful or handsome is.

By recognizing and addressing these seven areas, we can recalibrate our internal compass and navigate toward a more authentic and fulfilling life journey.

Chapter Three

Navigating Toward the Real You

*"I think everybody's weird. We should all
celebrate our individuality and not be
embarrassed or ashamed of it"*

—*Johnny Depp*

In the last chapter, we looked at all the different ways in which being inauthentic can affect your life, and how, when you are caught in the cycle of being someone you are not, change can feel daunting. However, there is good news!

You can always choose to change, embrace your true authentic self, and share it with the world, then you get to reap the rewards of simply being you!

Over the years of watching clients make changes, I've witnessed them become more relaxed within themselves and in the world around them, create deeper and more meaningful relationships, and start to notice new opportunities in all areas of their lives— leading to new careers, new relationships, travel, etc.

Once people rebuild their self-esteem and confidence, they begin to make choices and decisions for themselves that are in alignment with their values, and then they begin to live a life in which they experience satisfaction and fulfillment. You owe it to yourself to be you and experience everything that comes with it. No one else can do that for you; no one else, not even an identical twin, can be you.

I'm excited to share with you some powerful and practical strategies for change that are designed to target the areas for improvement that were highlighted with the acronym COMPASS. Subsequent chapters will explore and expand on each of the strategies below, and there are practical exercises to help you make the changes you need to make.

1. Tame the **C**omparison monster and develop a growth mindset.

You can do this by learning to:

- Practice gratitude for your unique journey.

- Limit social media exposure.

- Focus on personal growth rather than outperforming others.

- View challenges as opportunities to learn.

- Cultivate curiosity about yourself and the world.

- Prioritize self-care and establish consistent sleep, exercise, and nutrition habits.

2. Break the **O**verthinking Cycle.

To do this you can:

- Set aside dedicated "worry time."

- Practice mindfulness meditation.

- Use the "5-5-5" method: Will this matter in 5 days, 5 months, 5 years?

- Conquer "What if" thinking.

- Cultivate self-awareness by paying attention to your emotional reactions and triggers.

3. Realign your **M**isaligned values

Understanding your core values is the foundation of finding and maintaining your true self, so it is important to:

- Identify your core values.

- Regularly assess if your actions match your values.

- Make decisions based on your values, not external pressures.

- Engage in activities that bring you joy and relaxation.

4. Overcome **P**eople-pleasing tendencies and communicate assertively.

Establishing healthy boundaries and clear communication is essential for protecting your emotional well-being and maintaining authenticity. It's important to:

- Learn to say "no" without guilt.

- Set and communicate clear boundaries.

- Recognize that your needs are valid and important.

- Express your thoughts and feelings clearly and respectfully.

- Use "I" statements to own your emotions.

- Learn to disagree without being disagreeable.

5. Eliminate **A**voidance, embrace discomfort, and cultivate vulnerability. You can:

- Start with small challenges outside your comfort zone.

- Reframe discomfort as a sign of growth.

- Celebrate efforts, not just outcomes.

- Share your true feelings with a trusted friend or a therapist.

- Practice self-compassion.

- Recognize vulnerability as a strength, not a weakness.

- Learn to recognize and honor your emotional needs.

- Learn assertive communication.

6. Combat Self-doubt and build self-esteem. Some of the ways to do this are to:

- Release unhelpful or limiting beliefs.

- Keep a journal to document your successes and also for self-reflection.

- Challenge negative self-talk.

- Surround yourself with supportive, encouraging people.

- Discover and reinforce positive aspects of yourself.

- Recognize that mistakes are simply an opportunity to do it differently next time.

7. Resist Social conditioning and peer pressure and embrace imperfection.

To become comfortable simply being yourself, you will need to:

- Question societal norms and expectations.

- Become curious about different perspectives and experiences.

- Develop a strong sense of self; separate from group identity.

- Let go of unrealistic standards.

- Celebrate progress over perfection.

- Find beauty in your unique quirks and flaws.

- Surround yourself with authentic, supportive individuals.

- Join groups or communities that are aligned with your values.

In Chapter Two, I shared the story of Emma, who had a rhinoplasty and then realized that it didn't give her the confidence and self-esteem that she thought it would. In the weeks that followed this realization, Emma began a journey of self-discovery. She started working with me and discovered that she was constantly using what if thinking, such as:

"What if I'm not good enough?"

"What if they don't accept me?"

"What if they don't like me?"

"What if they think I have nothing to say?"

"What if I can't think of anything to say?" and much more!

She learned to challenge her negative self-talk and change her what if thinking.

Emma started working with the "I am" process to build a positive relationship with herself and her body. We elicited her values relating to career, relationships, and health and released unresolved negative emotions from the past, as well as clearing up limiting beliefs that were holding her back.

Emma took up activities she'd always been too insecure to try, like dance classes and public speaking workshops, and she began to build genuine confidence based on her abilities, values, and strengths rather than just her appearance.

It wasn't always easy; there were still days when Emma struggled with her appearance in the mirror. But over time, she learned to appreciate herself as a whole person, not just a collection of physical features to be critiqued and improved.

By the completion of our sessions, Emma was looking at her rhinoplasty as a turning point— not because it had given her the perfect nose but because it had taught her an invaluable lesson about true self-esteem. She'd learned that while changing her appearance could be empowering in the short term, real confidence and a true sense of self had to come from within.

There are so many benefits to being your authentic self, and these definitely outweigh any challenges you might face on the way to discovering and becoming your true self:

1. Real Friendships: When you're real, you attract people who like you for who you actually are, and you can have honest and open conversations even if you don't agree on a topic.

2. Less Stress: You don't have to remember which version of yourself you are to different people. You don't have to diminish yourself or play a role.

3. Feeling Better: When you are in alignment with your own values and beliefs, you will notice yourself feeling happier, more joyful, and experiencing more inner peace. One of my clients said, "It all comes from being aligned to who I am and what I want. Life is so much easier. I'm confident and strong. I can relate. I'm real."

4. Increased Confidence: The more you practice being the true you, the more comfortable you become in your own skin.

5. Better Decisions: When you're true to yourself, it's easier to have clarity and know what you want in life. You can trust that the choices you make are the right ones for you.

6. Inspiring Others: By being authentic, you inspire other people to be real too.

Remember, personal growth is a journey, not a destination. Be patient and kind to yourself as you work on these areas because authenticity and inner strength are muscles that grow stronger with consistent practice and self-compassion.

Are you ready to change?

Then head to the next chapter and let's get started!

Chapter Four

Tame the Comparison Monster

"Be yourself; everyone else is already taken."

—Oscar Wilde

C omparing ourselves to others is one of the main ways that self-esteem and the sense of self begin to falter. We are all unique individuals with a different way of perceiving and interpreting the world. Even members of the same family going through an event will all have a different perspective or story about what happened. What is right for one person is not necessarily right for another. When you are starting to regain or find your authentic self, it's important to stop the comparison to others and start to build a strong foundation in who you are, what you stand for, and what your likes and dislikes are. The only comparison that counts is looking at your own progress.

Limit Social Media Exposure

Some people spend a large amount of time on social media, seeing friends or acquaintances seemingly having a wonderful time traveling, going out for dinner, at parties, having fun, and looking fantastic, but what they don't realize is that they are viewing a snapshot in time, or a manufactured moment designed to portray something specific, and that the people they are viewing are not living these experiences 24/7. They, too, have times when they look tired, are doing it tough, feel emotional, or are experiencing something that is less than perfect, but we don't see this in the posts. In truth, you have no idea what their life is actually like.

The danger is that scrolling through posts, assuming everyone else is living a more fun, exciting, adventurous, happy, or interesting life, can leave you feeling isolated, disheartened, dissatisfied, or unhappy with your own life, and trying to compete with or outdo friends or acquaintances is like a dog chasing its tail; it's going to take a lot of time and energy but not achieve anything worthwhile.

Reducing your time on social media can lead to improved mental health, increased productivity, and an enhanced sense of well-being. Start by tracking your current social media usage using an app or built-in screen time monitors on your devices. Set specific time limits for social media use, such as 30 minutes per day, or 30 minutes twice per day in the weaning off phase, and stick to them. Consider implementing a "social media-free" day each week to break the habit of constant checking. Use app blockers or adjust your phone's settings to limit notifications and access to social media apps during certain hours. Replace scrolling time with more fulfilling activities like reading, exercising, having conversations with people, or pursuing a hobby.

When you do use social media, be intentional about it—engage meaningfully with friends and family rather than mindlessly scrolling, and scroll straight past ads and negative posts. Regularly audit your follow list and unfollow accounts that don't contribute positively to your life or mental state. Monitor your own posts and be mindful to not get caught in the habit of posing at every opportunity, trying to create a perfect image, recording every experience on social media, and not actually being present and living those experiences.

Focus On Personal Growth Rather Than Competing With Others

Shifting your focus from competition to personal development can lead to greater satisfaction and increased confidence. Start formulating a growth mindset by looking at skills and abilities as things that can be improved and built upon. Start saying "Yes" to experiences that interest you, even if your friends are not interested or don't agree. Say "No" to things you are doing just to please others or to try and fit in.

Cultivate curiosity about yourself and the world, as it can lead to a more fulfilling and engaging life. Some of my clients find that after the breakup of a marriage or death of a partner, they have no idea what their own likes and dislikes are because they've always listened to the music their partner likes, read the same things their partner read, did activities with their partner, or settled for eating the same foods as their partner. This can also happen when we hang out with friends; we go along with their choices and preferences rather than voicing our own, and eventually we lose ourselves. Do you have a friend or a partner who always responds with "I don't mind" when you ask where they want to go, what they want to do, or what they want to eat? Start to encourage them to make a choice, rather than making it for them.

If you are that person who says, "I don't mind," make a commitment to yourself to make a choice next time you are asked, step out of your comfort zone, and start to explore what you want in life.

To start finding out who you are and what you stand for, begin to read books or magazines in different genres; don't just do what you've always done! If you've always read nonfiction, read fiction; if you've never read a sci-fi book, start reading one; if you like it, great! If you don't like it, great! You've learned something about yourself! Then do the same with music. Explore different genres—classic, country, pop, rock, etc.—and evaluate them for yourself. It's fun to do this with food too; whether you check out some recipes and start exploring new things at home or order different dishes at restaurants than you normally would. As they say, "Variety is the spice of life."

Each week, set aside a little time for learning something new, whether it's through online courses, documentaries, YouTube videos, or go to a local cooking class, meditation class, golf lesson, art class, yoga class, public speaking group, or join a sport, etc.—the possibilities are endless. It doesn't matter where you start and what you do as long as you are challenging yourself and evaluating what resonates with you and what doesn't.

When you meet new people, practice asking open-ended questions rather than a question they can respond to with a "Yes" or "No." Have fun with conversations so that you can deepen your understanding of others and their different perspectives. Practice listening rather than jumping ahead in your mind, thinking of what to say next. If you take the time to listen, the conversation will flow much more easily and naturally.

Travel to new places, even if it's just exploring a different neighborhood in your city. Drive a different route home from work or go and visit the local tourist attractions to expose yourself to a variety of experiences. The more variety we have and the more small changes we make, the easier it becomes to make big ones. Embrace a beginner's mindset, approaching familiar situations with fresh eyes, curiosity, and a willingness to learn and explore.

Keep a "Discovery Journal" where you note what you think of the books you've read, music you've listened to, activities you've tried, or new food you've eaten. Use a separate page for each category, then make a note in your journal each time you read, listen to, or eat something different and evaluate what you liked and what you didn't—this is you discovering you! Remember, it's not about liking everything you try; it's about exploring new things and learning for yourself whether they resonate with you or not.

You can also use the journal to note improvements, positive moments, and successes—no matter how small—as this will help you to maintain motivation and also begin to see the positive changes you are making in your life. Celebrate your own achievements and milestones without comparing them to others. Remember that everyone's journey is unique, and success means something different for everyone. Focus on becoming a better version of yourself for yourself rather than trying to be better than someone else.

View Challenges as Opportunities to Learn

Reframing challenges as learning experiences can help you develop resilience and adaptability. Instead of flooding yourself with negative talk about what you don't have, didn't do, how you messed up, what's wrong about you, etc., take a deep breath... pause... and ask yourself, "What can I learn from this? How can I do it differently next time?" You might even want to make a note of difficulties you encountered, how you addressed them, and the learnings you gained, or what skills you need in order to handle a similar situation better in the future.

Remember that setbacks are a normal part of any growth process and don't define your worth or abilities. It's not about being or doing something perfectly, it's about being real. There are no failures; it's simply feedback so that you can do it differently in the future.

Practice Gratitude For Your Unique Journey

Cultivating gratitude for your personal journey can significantly enhance your overall well-being and perspective on life. Start by keeping a daily gratitude journal, where you write down three things you're happy or thankful for each day. These can be small moments, personal achievements, or aspects of your life you appreciate. Reflect on the challenges you've overcome and how they've shaped you into who you are today. When we stop trying to be like everyone else or do what everyone else is doing, we begin to discover the things we are happy or grateful for in our own life. Share your gratitude with others by expressing appreciation to friends, family, or colleagues regularly. This not only strengthens your relationships but also reinforces your own sense of thankfulness.

Prioritize Self-Care

You are your most valuable asset! On the journey of discovering yourself and being your best self for you—not for anyone else—it's important to prioritize your health and well-being. Start by establishing a consistent sleep schedule, aiming for 6–9 hours of sleep per night. Create a relaxing bedtime routine, such as reading or gentle stretching, to signal to your body that it's time to wind down. Keep devices and the TV out of the bedroom. You may find drinking herbal tea or taking a warm shower prior to bed helps you get to sleep. Ensuring your room is dark and cool also promotes better sleep.

To ensure you get physical exercise, find activities you enjoy and schedule them into your week like any other important appointment. You might decide to join a gym or go to some type of exercise class, learn to dance, or simply put on some uplifting music and dance around your home. Gardening can be great exercise, and if you don't have your own garden, you can find a local community garden that you can be part of. Look for ways to spend time in nature: walking, cycling, swimming, etc. You can also check out local "Meetup" groups for walking and other activities. Start small, even just 10–15 minutes a day, and gradually increase duration and intensity.

For nutrition, focus on eating a balanced diet that's right for your body. Do some meal prep on your days off to ensure you have healthy options readily available during busy workdays. Stay hydrated by keeping a water bottle with you and setting reminders to drink regularly throughout the day. Remember that self-care also includes mental and emotional aspects. Therefore it's important to practice stress-reduction techniques like meditation, deep breathing, self-hypnosis, or journaling.

Regularly assess your self-care routine and make adjustments as needed to ensure it continues to serve your evolving needs.

Taking time to look after your physical, mental, and emotional health is an important aspect of learning to love, value, and respect yourself. By decreasing social media time, you are making time available to improve your life and focus on things that expand you as a person and bring happiness and fulfillment.

Chapter Five

Break the Overthinking Cycle

"As you think, so shall you become."

—Bruce Lee

O verthinking things can be exhausting! Allowing yourself to ruminate about things is like a hamster on a wheel that just won't stop running. You might be thinking about things that people have said, making assumptions about what they mean, or you may be thinking that you're not good enough, not clever enough, or not as capable/talented as someone else... the list goes on!

When you are constantly overthinking things, the conclusions that you come to may be far from the actual reality. Your mind is great at making up stories, but that doesn't mean they are true!

Your unconscious mind, which is the part of your mind that runs your body, stores your memories, and houses your emotions, can't tell the difference between what you are thinking and what is actually happening. So, when you allow yourself to get caught up in running negative thoughts, your unconscious mind perceives that those scenarios are actually happening, secretes stress chemicals such as adrenaline and cortisol, and also tries to find solutions to the problems.

At the end of the day, you may be exhausted without having exerted yourself physically.

To slow it down, set aside a specific "worry window" for maybe twenty minutes each day when you give yourself permission to worry about everything that's bothering you. It's like scheduling a meeting with your worries instead of letting them interrupt you all day long. Outside this time, when worries pop up, you can tell them, "STOP" I'll deal with you during my "worry time" or write it down and focus back on the present moment instead. Think of this like making an appointment with your worries. Just like you wouldn't let someone randomly wander in and out of your office all day long, don't let worries interrupt you whenever they want. Pick a specific time (say 5–5.20 p.m.). When "worry time" comes, sit down and give those concerns your full attention. You might find that some worries that seemed huge in the morning don't even matter by the evening.

Negative thinking can also be in the form of "what-if" thoughts:

- What if this goes wrong?

- What if that doesn't work?

- What if that happens?

- What if.....?

A what-if thought is always a thought about something that hasn't happened yet and may never happen. For example, "What if I have a terrible day at work today and my boss is mean to me?" When we are doing what-if thinking, we usually don't stop at one thought; we run a myriad of them, and they can go on to produce anxiety.

The easiest way to start making changes with what-if thinking is to tell yourself, "STOP." Then ask yourself, "Do I have proof?" If not, let it go and turn it around to the exact positive opposite. (Ninety-nine percent of what-if thoughts have no proof.)

For example:

- ➢ What if? "What if I mess up my presentation at work tomorrow and they all think I'm stupid?"

- ➢ STOP. (Say it out loud if you are on your own.)

- ➢ Do I have proof? "Do I have proof right now this very minute that I will mess up my presentation?" ... "Well, actually no, because I'm not even at work yet."

- ➢ Turn it around. "What if I do a good job with the presentation?" (You may not believe this consciously. However, your unconscious mind needs to hear this positive turn around.)

Another example:

- ➢ What if?

- ➢ "What if my partner leaves me?"

> ➢ STOP.

> ➢ (Say it out loud if you are on your own.)

> ➢ Do I have proof?

> ➢ "Do I have proof right now this very minute that my partner is going to leave me?" ... "No, right now things are going well."

> ➢ Turn it around.

> ➢ "What if we continue to enjoy a great relationship?" (You may not believe this consciously. However, your unconscious mind needs to hear this positive turn around.)

When you overcome your what-if thinking, you will find yourself feeling much calmer and able to be more positive, as well as having a clearer mind.

Making Decisions

When you are unsure of yourself or you are making decisions to please others, analysis paralysis can happen. This is a state where you become so overwhelmed by analyzing a situation or decision that you become unable to take action. It's like trying to pick a movie on Netflix where you spend so much time reading reviews, comparing options, and worrying about making the "right" choice that you end up watching nothing at all. It's the mental gridlock that happens when overthinking prevents action.

Here Is How Analysis Paralysis Becomes A Cycle:

1. Initial Decision Point
↓
2. Begin Analysis
↓
3. Find More Factors to Consider
↓
4. Feel Overwhelmed by Information
↓
5. Seek More Data for Certainty
↓
6. Become More Confused/Anxious
↓
7. Avoid Making Decision
↓
8. Feel Bad About Not Deciding
↓
9. Start Process Again

To overcome analysis paralysis, you can adopt the "Two-Minute Rule."

If a decision will take less than two minutes of thought, make it immediately. For bigger decisions, set proportional time limits:

- Small decisions: 10 minutes max

- Medium decisions: 1 hour max

- Large decisions: 1 day max

- Life-changing decisions: 1 week max

With large or life-changing decisions, it can help to write a pros and cons list.

When you are learning to trust yourself and make decisions for yourself rather than what you think is acceptable to others, it's important to remember that:

1. Perfect decisions don't exist.

2. Action beats analysis.

3. Most decisions are reversible.

4. Learning comes from doing, and a "mistake" is simply feedback letting you know that you can do it differently next time.

The key is to start small and build confidence through practice. Every decision that you make is a step toward breaking the analysis paralysis cycle and being true to yourself. Focus on progress, not perfection, and congratulate yourself for having the courage to take action.

Practice Mindfulness Meditation

This isn't about becoming a Zen master; it's simply about learning to be present in the moment. Imagine your thoughts are like clouds passing through the sky of your mind. Instead of getting tangled up in each cloud, mindfulness teaches you to observe them floating by without getting caught up in the storm.

Teach yourself that a thought is not good, not bad, not important; it just is.... and let it pass (like a cloud passing through).

Start small. Even just focusing on your breathing for five minutes a day can help you develop this skill. When you notice your mind wandering, gently bring it back to your breath, like training a puppy to stay.

At times there may be so much going on in your mind that it seems impossible to be present. When that happens, another technique you can use is to look at something in your immediate vicinity; it could be a bookcase, a tree, a building, etc. Now begin to describe that object to yourself in great detail.

For example: The tree is medium height. It has lots of branches that are growing upward. The leaves on the branches are a variety of colors; some have a yellow tinge to them, others are medium green, and there are also some that are dark green. At the top of the tree, the canopy of leaves is very thick. At the bottom of the tree, several branches are bare. Some of these branches are hanging down; others are growing upward.

Once you have finished describing every minute detail to yourself, take a deep breath and notice how much calmer your mind is.

The 5-5-5 Method

This is a simple reality check for your worries. When something is bothering you, ask yourself: Will this matter in five days? Five months? Five years? For example, that embarrassing thing you said in a meeting might feel huge today, but in five days, people will probably have forgotten. That missed deadline might matter in five days, but will likely not matter in five months in terms of your work record, and in five years it will be irrelevant. This helps put your worries into perspective and saves your energy for things that truly matter long term.

Cultivating Self-Awareness

Think of self-awareness as becoming a detective of your own emotions. Pay attention to what triggers you. Maybe you notice you get anxious every Sunday evening before the work week, or perhaps you always feel inferior in a certain group, or feel as though you are never taken seriously by a certain person. By understanding these patterns, you can better prepare for them or address them directly. It's like having a weather radar for your emotions. When you can see the storm coming, you can prepare for it.

By using the tips and techniques in this chapter, you will be able to address and overcome the tendency to get caught in the trap of overthinking. You will feel calmer and more able to think clearly. Being able to make decisions for yourself without external validation is an important step in being your true self. The more choices and decisions you begin to make for yourself, the more you will be able to trust your own judgment. It's a fact of life that not every decision you make is going to turn out the way you thought or hoped it would (and that's okay! It's simply part of the growth process), but adapting and navigating through this often leads to new opportunities.

Chapter Six

Realign Your Misaligned Values

"The most powerful relationship you will ever have is the relationship with yourself."

—*Steve Maraboli*

What is a Value?

A value is what is important to us, for example, honesty, trust, happiness, love, etc. If you ask yourself the question, "What is important to me about.... ?" your answer will contain values such as "Honesty is important to me."

Your values affect how you see the world and navigate through life. They're like invisible filters that affect goals and outcomes you set for yourself and the choices and decisions you make. They motivate actions, and they determine what you achieve, what you spend your time and energy on, how you perceive yourself (identity), and how you develop as an individual. Simply put, your values are the driving force behind your actions—they're why you do what you do. For example, if you value family above all else, you might make career choices that give you more time at home. If you value achievement, you might spend more time working toward professional goals. These choices shape who you become, how you see yourself, and the kind of person you grow into over time.

Values are like the foundation of a house—everything else in your life is built on top of them. Understanding your values helps you make choices that feel right for you and lead to a more satisfying life that matches what truly matters to you.

Where Do Values Come From?

Values can originate from family or friends, religion, school, geographical location, culture, economic position, the media, a mentor, etc.

Some values can be tied to a specific time, for example, "The moment it happened, I decided honesty does pay," or they can be tied to a specific person, perhaps because of something they said to you.

In situations where you have "lost yourself," you may find that you have adopted certain values of the person or people you are trying to please, either to be like them or to keep the peace.

Identifying misaligned values that are no longer beneficial enables us to change them to something that will work for you.

Identifying Your Core Values

I recommend identifying your values in the major areas of your life so that you can understand what is driving you. These areas are:

Work & Career	Relationships
Family	Health & Fitness
Social life	Personal development
Hobbies & Interests	Spirituality

Exercise:

Let's begin discovering your core values. Start with Work & Career. (If this is not relevant to you, go on to another one, e.g., Family).

At the top of a page in your journal, write: Work & Career.

Now ask yourself, "What's important to me about Work & Career?"

Write down anything and everything that comes to mind. Once you hit a blank, ask yourself the same question again: "What's important to me about Work & Career?"

Write down anything else that comes to mind, and when you hit a blank, ask the question again: "What's important to me about Work & Career?" Note anything else that comes up for you and then ask one last time, "What's important to me about Work & Career?" Doing this four times will help you to uncover more values each time.

Once they're listed, begin to rank your list in order of importance, and place a number one next to the item that's most important to you and continue ranking the rest of them in order of their importance.

Don't spend too much time thinking about it; go with whatever feels right. Make sure you are ranking them in order of what you **do** consider most important, not what "should" be most important.

No matter how long your list (you might have ten values), your top five values (highest ranked) are your core values and will drive everything you do. If they are not satisfied, you will feel unhappy, dissatisfied, unfulfilled, and may even have a sense of discomfort or unease.

Now, think about your work or career in the last twelve months and ask yourself if each of your top five values was fulfilled during this time. If not, this will be the reason why you have been feeling unhappy, dissatisfied, or unfulfilled. It's important to look at how you can satisfy those values either by making some adjustments in your current position or by looking for new work.

Do this same process for all the areas of your life listed above, and discover the core values that are driving every part of your life. If there are core values that you would like to change, this can be done with the help of a hypnotherapist or NLP (neuro-linguistic programming) practitioner.

Remember the story of Simon I shared with you in Chapter Two? Here are Simon's values in relation to his career:

1. Respect

2. Creativity

3. Validation

4. Fun

5. Financial Security

6. Work/life balance

7. Autonomy

8. Growth

His core values are numbers one through five above. We can see that his need for the boss to "like and value him" stems from those core values, as does his need to "be a good provider." His number two value is creativity and that was not fulfilled at all in his career, and neither was fun. Once Simon was aware of this, he had to decide what to do in order to fill his need for creativity and fun.

Making Decisions Based on Your Values, Not External Pressures

When you begin to make decisions based on your personal values, it's like having a strong filter to guide your decisions. Keep a list of your top five values in each context in your phone so it's always close by.

When facing a decision, pause and ask yourself:

- Am I doing this for myself or to please others?

- Does this align with my top five values?

- Will I feel good about this choice in the long run?

You may want to put these questions in your phone as your go-to whenever you need to make a decision.

Say "No" to things that don't align with your values. For example, if your top five values for work are:

1. Working in a supportive environment

2. Family time

3. Flexibility

4. Autonomy

5. Opportunities for growth

..... but you're considering taking a job just for money and prestige; that's a misalignment with your values, as money and prestige are not represented in your top five. If you took the job, you would find yourself feeling unhappy quite quickly.

Regularly assess if your actions match your values by setting a monthly "values check-in" with yourself. In your journal or in a note-taking app, keep a note of:

- Choices where you felt drained or resentful (these were choices that went against your values).

- Choices that were aligned with your values and how that felt.

By looking at this each month, you'll see patterns emerge that can guide your future decisions.

Engage in Activities That Bring Joy and Relaxation

This is about intentionally creating space for what truly makes you happy.

1. Make a Joy Inventory. Include simple pleasures and bigger experiences. Start

by listing twenty things that bring you genuine joy—not what should make you happy, but what actually does. These could be simple things like reading in the morning sun, taking a long bath, or cooking your favorite meal.

- Identify what truly helps you to unwind.

- List activities that you become so engaged in you lose track of time.

- Note what activities energize rather than drain you.

2. Schedule these activities deliberately. Intentionally incorporate these into your daily routine. Start with one joyful activity daily.

- Block out time in your calendar for joyful activities.

- Treat these appointments with the same importance as work meetings.

- Start with small, regular doses (even fifteen minutes counts). For example, if you love music, start each day with one favorite song. If nature brings you peace, take a short walk during your lunch break.

Practical Application

Let's say, like Simon, "creativity" is one of your core values, but you're spending all your time in a purely analytical job. You could:

1. Start with fifteen minutes of creative time each morning.

2. Join a weekend art class.

3. Look for ways to bring creative thinking into your current work.

4. Consider long-term career adjustments that better align with creativity.

Then, plan a new schedule that better reflects your values. If health is important to you but you're not exercising, block out specific times for movement. If family time is crucial but work is consuming all your time, schedule non-negotiable family time.

The key is to make these changes sustainable rather than trying to overhaul your entire life at once. Small, consistent steps in alignment with your values will lead to significant positive changes in your life satisfaction, self-esteem, and sense of self. Be patient with yourself and celebrate progress!

Chapter Seven

Overcome People Pleasing, Set Boundaries, & Communicate Assertively

"You can never be happy living someone else's dream. Live your own. And you will for sure know the meaning of happiness."

—Oprah Winfrey

An important part of being your true self and overcoming the tendency to please others is to be able to communicate clearly, know what your boundaries are, and enforce them. This enables you to live a happier life.

Setting Boundaries

Boundaries are like your personal property line; they show where you end and others begin. Clear boundaries protect your mental and emotional well-being. They teach others how to treat you. If you are not being your true self, you are not protecting and enforcing your boundaries, and therefore people are not likely to value or respect you. When you are constantly trying to please others, you are allowing their needs to be more important than your own and are setting aside your boundaries. It is important to realize that your needs matter just as much as anyone else's. If you've ever traveled on a plane, you know that they instruct you to put an oxygen mask on yourself first before helping others. In life, it is important to fulfill your own needs first, and then you will have the resources and energy to be able to help others.

The people pleaser is often a person who is kindhearted and generous and will say "Yes" to helping others to their own detriment, or they are someone who wants to be loved, liked, respected, or valued and believes that saying "Yes" to others will get them the recognition they are seeking. Sadly, it sets up the opposite! When you don't love, like, respect, or value yourself by enforcing your boundaries and saying "No" to the things that are not right for you, others won't respect you either.

In the story about Simon, in Chapter Two, I mentioned that he always said "Yes" to anything his boss asked him to do. If he was asked to work late or on the weekend, he would say "Yes," automatically, even if that meant he lost out on time with his wife and kids. Simon always said "Yes" to extra work because he thought his boss would value and respect him, and therefore his position would be safe.

One of Simon's top five values is financial security, and so it was important to him to have the security of his job. I explained to him that if you always say "Yes," people do not respect you; in fact, they don't even have to think about you! Each time a task needed to be done, the boss already knew Simon would do it, so she would just hand over the task, no matter what it was, secure in the knowledge that "Simon will do this, Simon will fix this, Simon will stay back and take care of that, Simon will work the weekends, no problem!" and no consideration was given as to whether Simon could handle the workload or work the extra hours.

So, Simon's boss didn't even have to think or question whether he could do a task; she just handed it off to him, fully expecting it to be done. Once you learn to say "No," the other person has to think more about you. They have to consider if you will be able to assist. "I wonder if Simon can do this? I hope Simon can help at the weekend."

If you say "No" (in this case to the boss), that person has to either do the task themselves, or delegate it to someone else. They become responsible for the issue/task themselves and from that point onward, they will begin to acknowledge and respect the times when you do say "Yes."

When we talked about boundaries, Simon was able to see how he had enabled his boss to take advantage of him. Saying "No" to things that were not aligned with his values or didn't respect his boundaries became very important to him.

Learning to Say "No" Without Guilt

Think of your time and energy like a bank account—you only have so much to spend. When you say "Yes" to one thing, you're saying "No" to something else. When you say "Yes" to something that's not right for you, it's like telling yourself that you don't count, and your self-esteem starts to drop. If you go ahead and do that activity anyway, you will find that you don't enjoy it, you may feel resentful, and the stress builds up. Saying "No" isn't selfish; it's self-care.

Learning to say "No" is easier than you think. There are three questions (criteria) to ask yourself before saying "Yes," or "No." Always give yourself the opportunity to run these questions before you respond to someone.

The questions are:

1. "Do I want to?"

2. "Do I personally need to?"

3. "For what purpose would I do this?"

If the answers are:

1. "No, I don't want to."

2. "I do not personally need to."

3. "The purpose is purely because someone else wants/needs/expects it"

then say, "No!"

Many people find it difficult to say, yet it's only a two-letter word! Once you learn how to say

"No," you will wonder why you haven't been doing this for years!

To say "No" ... get the "No" out first.

"No, thank you for asking. I really can't help."

"No, thank you for asking. I can't come."

Repeat this like a broken record if the other person continues to ask why, etc. If you give reasons or make excuses, the other person has information to manipulate you with, for example:

Boss: "Can you write the report for XYZ on Saturday?"

Simon: "Sorry, I don't have time. I have to take the kids to sports practice."

Boss: "That's okay. I'll make arrangements for you to have access to it from home."

If Simon had said, "No, thank you for asking. I really can't help," the boss would have no information to manipulate him with.

Simon thought he was saying "No" by telling his boss, "Sorry, I don't have time. I have to take the kids to sports practice." However, his boss simply ignored this because there was not a firm "No," and arranged for it to be done from home.

I explained to Simon that the word "No" needs to be clear. This is why we say it first. "No!" The "thank you for asking" helps the "No" response to be easily accepted. If the person continues to ask, simply repeat, "No, thank you for asking. I can't help." With no other details or explanation, the "No" will eventually be accepted.

The following week, when his boss asked him to stay back and work on a project, Simon ran the questions through his mind.

"Do I want to?... No!"

"Do I personally need to?... No!"

"For what purpose would I do this?... Because my boss expects it"

... so he replied, "No, thank you for asking. I really can't help."

The boss looked at him and said, "Okay, I'll get John to do it" and continued with the conversation. Simon was amazed at just how easy it was to say "No."

Several months later he reported back to me that his work life was much more balanced, he had time to have fun with his wife and kids, he had started to take an evening art class, and he found that saying "No" to his boss on several occasions had led to a positive change in attitude from her.

Now, sometimes, when you ask the three questions:

1. "Do I want to?"

2. "Do I personally need to?"

3. "For what purpose would I do this?"

the answers could be:

1. "No, I don't want to."

2. "Yes, I do personally need to."

3. "The purpose is (a benefit) for me."

In this case, even though the "want to" is a "No," there is a positive benefit for you in the answers. Therefore, the right thing would be to go ahead and do it.

For example:

"Do I want to go for a walk today?"

"No, I don't want to."

"Do I personally need to go for a walk today?"

"Yes, I probably do."

"For what purpose would I go for a walk today?"

"Because I haven't been for one this week, and I want to stay healthy."

When we consciously realize that there is a positive to doing the activity, even though the "Do I want to?" was "No," we find ourselves undertaking that activity with a motivated frame of mind, and there is no resentment or stress building under the surface.

Exercise:

What things or people do you have difficulty saying "No" to?

Run a few examples for yourself and practice giving the "No" response next time you are asked:

> "(Your name), can you help me with this/do this/come?"

Ask yourself the questions and write your answers:

> Do I want to?

> Do I personally need to?

> For what purpose would I do this?

> Then practice: "No, thank you for asking. I really can't help you with that/do that/come."

Start with a small no, maybe declining an invitation to an event you don't want to attend—and build up to the bigger ones. It can feel scary or uncomfortable the first few times you say "No," but persevere because, in a very short period of time, you will have more time to do the things that you want to do, and you will notice your self-esteem increasing as you begin to assert, respect, and value yourself. You will also begin to realize that the people around you respect you for being able to say "No."

When you are establishing your boundaries:

1. Identify your non negotiables (what behaviors are okay/not okay): For example, "I need at least one hour of alone time daily," "I don't check work emails after 6 p.m."

2. Communicate them clearly: "I don't check work emails or take work calls after 6 p.m."

3. Be consistent in enforcing them.

4. Start with one boundary and add more as you get comfortable.

5. Practice asking for what you need in minor situations first.

Communicating Assertively

Many people confuse assertive behavior with aggressive behavior. Aggressiveness involves expressing thoughts, feelings, and beliefs in a way that is inappropriate and communicates disrespect. Assertiveness can be defined as "behavior which enables us to communicate our needs, preferences, opinions, and feelings to other people in an effective way without violating the rights of others." An assertive person has respect for themselves and others. They can express their thoughts, feelings, needs, and beliefs more openly and honestly and are able to listen, negotiate, and compromise. If you feel as though you have lost your voice or haven't been able to speak your truth for any reason, then this section is vital for you! It's time to find your voice and express yourself clearly! Remember that your thoughts, opinions, needs, and desires are just as important as anyone else's.

Expressing Thoughts and Feelings Clearly and Respectfully

Clear communication is like being a good translator—you're helping others to understand your internal world. The intention is to be honest while maintaining respect for yourself and others. A powerful way to do this is to use "I" statements such as:

"I feel _____ "

"I need _____ "

"I want _____ "

"I'd like_____ "

Using "I" Statements to Own Your Emotions

"I" statements put you in the driver's seat of your emotions. When you use a "You" statement, the other person's defenses are activated. So, instead of saying "You make me angry," say "I feel angry when..." This approach takes ownership of your feelings while reducing the other person's defensiveness.

"I" statement format:

1. "I feel _____" (emotion)

2. "when_____" (specific situation)

3. "because ____" (impact on you) *(optional step)*

4. "I need _____" (requested change) or

"I want _____" or "I'd like _____"

Example: "I feel overwhelmed and stressed when meetings run late because it affects my family time. I need us to stick to scheduled end times."

Or: "I feel overwhelmed and stressed when meetings run late. I need us to stick to scheduled end times."

Learning to Disagree Without Being Disagreeable

Think of disagreement like dancing—you can step on someone's toes, or you can move gracefully together even when going in different directions. The goal is to be able to express different viewpoints while keeping respect and rapport.

How to disagree respectfully:

1. Stay calm, use a normal conversational tone, and keep your facial expressions neutral.

2. Listen fully before responding and briefly summarize their point.

3. Acknowledge the other person's perspective first, e.g., "I respect your point of view."

4. Use phrases like "I see it differently" or "I have a different perspective" instead of "You're wrong"

5. Focus on facts rather than emotions.

6. Look for common ground.

7. Stay focused on solutions rather than problems.

"I respect your point of view that dogs make the best companions. However, I see it differently. Cats can be loyal and loving companions too. It's great that we both love our pets, and I'm hopeful we can grow to like each other's pets."

Warning signs you're getting disagreeable:

- Your voice gets louder.

- You start interrupting.

- You use words like "never" and "always."

- You bring up unrelated issues.

- Your heart begins to race.

- You stop listening and just wait for your turn to speak.

If this happens, take a few deep breaths, regroup, and calm yourself, and let the other person know. Say, "I'm feeling overwhelmed and need a break for ten minutes," as continuing the conversation in that state will not be productive.

Useful Phrases to Practice:

"I see things differently, and here's why..."

"I value our relationship, and I need to be honest about..."

"I wonder if we could explore this from another angle?"

"I respect your view and ...."

"I appreciate... and ...."

How to Practice Assertive Communication

1. Before important conversations, write down your main points.

2. Use specific examples instead of generalizations.

3. Focus on current situations rather than past grievances.

4. Write it out using the "I" statements.

5. Practice in low-risk situations first.

Exercise:

Think of a recent situation where you could have implemented a boundary or expressed your opinion more assertively. Write it out using the "I" format:

> "I feel (emotion) _____ "

> when (specific situation) _____ "

> because (impact on you) _____ "

> "I need/I want/I'd like (requested change) _____ "

Think of developing these skills like building muscle—start small, be consistent, and gradually increase the challenge. It might feel uncomfortable at first but with practice, it becomes more natural. It's important to start practicing your new skills in safe relationships first before using them in more challenging ones. Be patient with yourself and celebrate the wins, no matter how small. Remember that you're not just learning new skills; you're establishing a new way of showing up in the world that honors both yourself and others.

Chapter Eight

Eliminate Avoidance, Embrace Discomfort, & Cultivate Vulnerability

"Vulnerability is the key that unlocks the door to growth and fulfillment."

—*Tony Robbins*

If you have been hiding some part of your true self, then it's likely you have been using avoidance strategies. Avoidance is like an invisible shield that you use to protect yourself from uncomfortable feelings, situations, or truths about yourself.

One of my clients, James, knew deep down that he was unhappy in his career, but rather than do anything about it, he filled every moment of the day being so busy that he avoided thinking about it. Whenever friends asked whether he was happy or enjoyed his job, James changed the subject and avoided answering. Frequently, he would spend hours scrolling through social media rather than updating his résumé, or he would make excuses about it "not being the right time" to make a change.

When someone isn't living authentically, avoidance often shows up as:

- Distracting themselves from their true feelings with activities, video games, shopping, addictive behaviors, work, exercise, etc.

- Making choices based on what's comfortable rather than what's true for them.

- Staying in situations that don't align with their values because change feels scary.

- Putting up a false front to please others while hiding their real self.

The tricky thing about avoidance is that it might feel like it's protecting you in the short term, but over time, it can lead to feeling disconnected from yourself and your genuine desires.

Start with Small Challenges Outside Your Comfort Zone

To break the pattern of avoidance, it's important to start by gradually facing whatever it is you've been avoiding. To do this, sit quietly and think about what you're avoiding. For example: "Why am I so unhappy in my job (body, relationship, etc.)?" "Why can't I be myself around my friends (family, etc.)?"

Exercise:

1. Make a list of the things that make you uncomfortable, then rank them from least to most challenging.

2. Decide to take one small action step toward change each day.

Begin with small challenges that make you slightly uncomfortable but aren't overwhelming, such as:

- Smiling at a stranger.

- Giving a genuine compliment.

- Sharing a minor opinion in a group.

- Asking for help with something small.

- Saying "No" to a minor request.

- Speaking up in a meeting at work when you would normally stay quiet.

- Sharing a small truth with someone safe.

- Trying something new on your own.

For example:

- If you're shy, you could start by making eye contact and smiling at one stranger per day, then build up to saying "Hello" and eventually to having brief conversations.

- If you can't be yourself around your friends because you think they will judge you or not like you because you dislike football and they all love it, tell them honestly, "I love hanging out with you all. However, I'm going to give the football game a miss this week as it's not really my thing. I'm sorry I wasn't honest about that earlier. I can't wait to catch up for drinks on Friday, though."

- If your friends are all dressing up in the same outfit for a theme night and you don't want to wear the outfit because as a plus-size person you feel uncomfortable in it, let them know. "I'm really looking forward to the party. You all look fabulous in the outfit. However, I feel more comfortable wearing _____."

- Visit a restaurant you've always wanted to go to by yourself.

- Invite a friend to an activity that you enjoy rather than always saying "Yes" to whatever they enjoy.

- Take the first step toward changing the job that you are unhappy with.

Practice self-awareness by keeping a journal to track your patterns of avoidance so that you become aware of them. Notice when you're using distractions (phone, TV, substances, food, overworking) and ask yourself, "What am I really feeling right now?" This will help you uncover the underlying emotions. Practice sitting with the uncomfortable feelings for just a few minutes; allow yourself to explore the feelings and then write them down.

It can also be beneficial to find a therapist, such as a hypnotherapist, to help you release unresolved emotions and teach you some powerful relaxation skills.

Reframing Discomfort as a Sign of Growth

Discomfort is like the slight soreness you get after exercising—it might not feel good in the moment, but it's a sign that you're getting stronger. When you are attempting something new and taking steps to show your true self, you might experience discomfort at first, like a fluttering in your stomach or tension in your chest. Rather than running from the discomfort, allow yourself to get curious about it.

Instead of thinking, "This feels awful; I want to stop," or what-if thoughts like "What if___ happens?" ask yourself, "What's this feeling trying to tell me?" Turn your focus on the positive outcome of what you are moving toward, not just on what you're avoiding.

Then tell yourself, "This feeling means I'm growing! It's a sign that I'm getting stronger" or "This is just growth happening, and it's good that I'm changing."

Welcome the discomfort as, over time, what once felt overwhelming becomes your new normal, and then you're ready for bigger challenges.

Cultivating Vulnerability

Being vulnerable means letting your guard down and showing your true self, even the parts you're not so proud of. It might be telling a close friend about your struggles with self-doubt or admitting to your partner that you're feeling lost in your career. The trick is to start with people who have earned your trust—those who've shown they can handle your truth with care. If you don't have anyone you can trust, find a therapist you feel comfortable with. Start with small disclosures to safe people, share a minor worry or insecurity, and notice how it feels to be heard and supported.

When you share something personal and feel exposed, treat yourself like you would a good friend. Instead of beating yourself up with thoughts like "I shouldn't have said that" or "They must think I'm stupid," tell yourself, "It took courage to open up" or "It's okay to not have it all figured out." Vulnerability isn't a flaw or a weakness—it's emotional courage, and it's what truly helps you build genuine connections with others. Yes, you might get hurt, but it's also the only way to let in love, connection, and growth. Begin to notice how sharing affects your relationships positively and gradually increase your emotional openness as your confidence grows.

The most respected leaders, closest friendships, and strongest relationships aren't built on pretending to be perfect. They're built on the courage to be real, to admit mistakes, to admit that we don't know something, and to show that we're all human. Being vulnerable means being brave enough to be seen as you truly are. Every time you choose to be vulnerable, you're not just helping yourself; you're giving others permission to feel safe and be authentic too.

Practicing Self-Compassion

Self-compassion is like being your own best friend. When you make a mistake or face a challenge, it's important to speak to yourself with the same kindness you'd offer a loved one, instead of the harsh self-criticism that people often engage in when they are out of alignment with themselves.

Most people are familiar with the notion that we have a conscious mind and an unconscious (subconscious) mind. Your unconscious mind is the part of you that is responsible for controlling your automatic bodily functions such as breathing, heartbeat, and blinking. It is also responsible for storing your memories. It houses your values, beliefs, and emotions, and it's the part of you that you don't have to think about.

The unconscious mind is creative, intuitive, irrational, and emotional. Because it's illogical, it can imagine anything you want, for example, wealth, health, and mood. It can also keep you stuck in negative behaviors if you continue to run negative belief patterns.

Your unconscious mind operates on its programming like a computer does, and it can be reprogrammed just like a computer. We are constantly reprogramming our unconscious mind through our experiences and self-talk. If we repeatedly tell ourselves that we are a failure or that we are a success, that we are happy or that we are anxious, that is what we become. What we tell ourselves, we become!

The conscious mind accounts for approximately ten percent of your mind. It's the part of you that's aware of what's going on right now. The conscious mind is logical and analytical, and it's where we spend most of our time. The conscious mind exercises willpower and analyzes and evaluates whatever concern, situation, or issue has its attention. It is with our conscious mind that we make decisions and choices. However, those decisions are influenced by the information stored in our unconscious mind.

I like to use the metaphor of the unconscious mind being just like a five-year-old child in how it acts and reacts to things. I liken the conscious mind to being a big brother or sister. Using harsh/unkind self-talk affects the five-year-old (unconscious mind). It creates beliefs and affects mood and ultimately behavior. Therefore, anything you say to yourself needs to be suitable enough to say to a five-year-old and have them feel happy and healthy. Thinking of the unconscious mind in this way helps us to easily make changes.

When you are out of alignment or hiding part of yourself, you might be using harsh and unkind self-talk, such as:

"I'm not good enough."

"I'm ugly."

"I'm not intelligent enough."

"I'm not likeable."

Imagine telling a five-year-old child:

"What if you have a terrible day at school today and nobody wants to play with you?"

"You're not as smart or as good-looking as the other kids."

"Everyone else does things better than you!"

That child certainly isn't going to want to go to school today, and if they do go, after you've told them all that, they're likely to have a very rough day!

We think nothing of telling ourselves things like this repeatedly, day in, day out, in our own minds, and then we wonder why we feel anxious, less worthy than others, or lack confidence in certain situations. In order to embrace your true self, it's important that you are kind to yourself. Monitor your internal dialogue—remember that if you can't say something out loud to a five-year-old child and have them feel happy and healthy, you can't say it to yourself. This is one of the easiest ways to keep your self-talk in check.

When you notice yourself being harsh, simply turn it around. For example:

"I'm not good enough."	Turn it around ...	"I am good enough."

"I'm not smart enough."	Turn it around …	"I am smart enough."

Your conscious mind may not believe the "turn it around" phrase. However, your unconscious mind needs to hear it!

Write your own examples in your journal:

I'm not _____

Now turn it around:

I am _____

The turn it around phrase is also great to use as an affirmation. Write it on a sticky note, attach it to your mirror, and read it every morning and every evening. Put the affirmation on your desk, in your wallet, on the back of your work ID badge—anywhere where you will be reminded of it regularly.

In addition to using critical self-talk, you may also be using language that puts pressure on yourself and creates stress. Replacing this language with any of the words of choice opens us up to possibilities.

Pressure	Choice
I should	I can
I must	I might
I ought to	I wonder what it would be like to
I have to	I wonder if I can
I've got to	Let's see
	It will be nice to

Notice the difference in these statements:

Pressure: "I have to run five miles on the treadmill today."

Choice: "Let's see if I can run five miles on the treadmill today."

Pressure: "I should finish the reports by lunchtime."

Choice: "It will be nice to finish the reports by lunchtime."

Pressure: "I've got to get the groceries on the way home."

Choice: "I can pick up the groceries on the way home."

Think of a time you have used these words of pressure and then reframe them to words of choice:

Pressure: "I (should, must, ought to, have to)

_____ "

Choice: "I can, I might, I wonder what it would be like to, I wonder if I can, let's see, it will be nice to

_____."

Write more examples in your journal so that you become familiar with replacing these words in your mind. If you use these words of pressure regularly, make an effort to remove them from your vocabulary and use words of choice instead.

In the following example I am aware that five-year-olds would not go to the gym or lift weights. However, you are learning to talk to yourself the way you would speak to a five-year-old regardless of context.

Michael, one of my clients, thought he was doing the right thing for his health and well-being by going to the gym daily, lifting weights and running on the treadmill. Some of his friends were triathletes, and he felt as though he needed to be as fit as they were to be accepted by them. We discovered that Michael was using words of pressure whilst at the gym:

"I should be lifting heavier weights."

"I have to do at least ten miles on the treadmill today."

"I have to do twenty repetitions today!"

"I've got to get fitter."

Then he would scold himself if he did not live up to his expectations, telling himself he was useless, weak, his friends wouldn't want to hang out with him, etc.

Now imagine for a moment telling a five-year-old:

"You should be lifting heavier weights."

"You have to do at least ten miles on the treadmill today." "You have to do twenty repetitions today!" "You've got to get fitter," and then telling him he is useless, weak, and no one will want to be his friend! That five-year-old won't want to go to the gym and certainly will not be having any fun! Now imagine saying to the five-year-old, "It might be fun to lift heavier weights today." "Let's see if we can do ten miles on the treadmill today." "I wonder if we can do twenty repetitions today." "You did a great job; you're getting better at it; you're awesome!" It's a very different feeling when you use words of choice and positive language.

Learning to Recognize and Honor Emotional Needs

Emotions are a normal and natural part of being human. They provide important information about your needs. It's time to start paying attention to your emotions and what they're telling you about your needs.

Learning to honor your emotional needs begins with the gentle practice of turning inward and becoming aware of what you are feeling.

Start by creating quiet moments in your day to check in with yourself, asking, "What am I feeling?" and more importantly, "What do I need right now?"

As you build this relationship with yourself, you'll begin to recognize your **emotional signals**:

- Tension in your shoulders might mean you need boundaries.

- A knot in your stomach might mean you need to speak your truth.

- A feeling of restlessness might mean you need to express your creativity.

Your **emotional needs** could be:

- Needing alone time to recharge.

- Setting limits with loved ones.

- Expressing yourself even when it feels vulnerable.

Remember that your feelings are valid messengers, not inconveniences to be pushed aside. When you catch yourself dismissing your emotions or automatically saying "Yes" when you mean "No" pause and acknowledge your true feelings. Taking care of your emotional well-being is a necessary act of self-respect that allows you to show up more authentically in all your relationships. As you practice tuning in to your emotions and emotional needs, you'll find yourself making choices that align with your true needs rather than simply meeting others' expectations.

Sarah was married to Mick. They had three grown-up children, and she had spent the last thirty-two years organizing and supporting everyone else's lives while her own dreams gathered dust in the corners of her mind. She came to see me after she found herself crying in the grocery store parking lot over a chicken Mick had asked her to pick up, even though she was just heading to her first yoga class in decades. Of course, it wasn't about the chicken. It was about the weight of all the times she had made sacrifices or compromises, all the times she had negated her own needs to maintain household harmony. The yoga class had been her first step, a tiny rebellion against her usual routine of arranging her schedule around everyone else's convenience.

As a result of our sessions, Sarah began to listen to the whispers of discontent she'd been silencing for years. She became aware of the emotions she was stuffing down in order to keep the peace or to always be there for others. At home, she began setting gentle boundaries, telling her family, "I need this hour for myself," or "I'd like to choose the restaurant tonight."

The first few times Sarah did this she found herself trembling. However, her voice got stronger each time. Her family's reactions surprised her. While there was initial confusion—Mick's puzzled expression when she declined to host his office party, her daughter's surprise when Sarah said "No" to babysitting—they began to adapt.

Sarah discovered needs she hadn't known existed:

- The need for solitude that led her to create a meditation space in the guest room.

- The need for adventure that inspired her to join a meetup hiking group.

- The need to follow her dream of becoming a yoga teacher.

Sarah shared her progress with me:

- She declined a committee position at church without offering an excuse.

- She expressed her preference to stay home over Mick's beloved weekend errands.

- Simply sitting in the backyard with her morning coffee instead of immediately starting the day's tasks.

At fifty-five, Sarah wasn't becoming a different person; she was finally becoming herself. Her marriage didn't crumble as she'd feared; instead, it deepened as Mick got to know this more authentic version of his wife. Her relationships with her children shifted from constant giving to mutual respect and appreciation as they began to see her not just as a wife, mother, and grandmother but as a person with her own dreams and desires.

Approximately nine months after our sessions ended, I ran into Sarah at the grocery store. She was picking up a chicken for Mick! She laughed as she told me that now if she did pick up a chicken for him, it was because she wanted to, not because she felt she had to. She said that in finding the courage to honor her needs, she had discovered the joy of being unapologetically herself.

Celebrating Efforts, Not Just Outcomes

On the journey to discovering yourself and having the courage to be authentic, success isn't just about reaching goals—it's about recognizing the courage it takes to make changes. If you only celebrate perfect outcomes, you become afraid to take risks. Instead, celebrate every attempt at becoming your true self, regardless of the result. The fact that you are attempting to do things differently means you are changing. Make sure you acknowledge yourself daily for stepping out of your old comfort zones and regularly give yourself small rewards for taking action.

Chapter Nine

Combat Self-Doubt and Build Self-Esteem

"Your self-worth is determined by you. You don't have to depend on someone telling you who you are."

—Beyoncé Knowles-Carter

Building genuine self-esteem from the ground up is like constructing a building—it requires a solid foundation and careful attention to detail, time, and patience. Every experience, every small victory, and even the setbacks become bricks in the foundation, contributing to a structure that can weather life's storms with resilience and grace.

Authentic self-esteem grows from a place of self-understanding and acceptance. It begins with recognizing that your worth isn't tied to your achievements, your appearance, or others' approval. It stems from a deeper appreciation of your inherent value as a human being, complete with your unique experiences, perspectives, and potential for growth.

The shift in perspective from seeing yourself as someone who has to constantly prove their worth to understanding that you are inherently worthy marks the beginning of true self-esteem.

Understanding the Root of Self-Doubt

Self-doubt often stems from deeply ingrained beliefs that we've accumulated throughout our lives. These beliefs act like filters, coloring our perception of ourselves and our capabilities. The first step in combating self-doubt is recognizing that these beliefs are not immutable truths; they are simply stories we've learned to tell ourselves.

Have you ever caught yourself thinking, *I'm not good at cooking,* or *I'll never be successful?* These thoughts might feel like facts, but they're actually limiting beliefs, and these invisible chains hold us back from reaching our full potential. They are the stories we tell ourselves about who we are, what we can and can't do, and what's possible in our lives.

Examples of limiting beliefs:

- Anything you "don't feel," e.g., "I'm useless," "I'm worthless" (implies "I don't feel useful/worthy)," "I don't (feel I) deserve good things," "I'm not capable," "I don't feel loved."

- "I can't" statements, such as "I can't be something/do something/have something, e.g., "I can't make enough money," "I can't dance," "I can't have what I want," and "I'm too old to start a new career" (implies "I can't start a new career)."

- When you make an absolute statement with always/never, e.g., "I never win things," "I always mess things up," "I never get picked for the team," "I never get a raise," "I always get the worst seat on the plane," "I always get the worst jobs at work," "I'll never find a partner."

- If you constantly compare yourself to others and come up short thinking they have something you don't, it's likely to be a limiting belief, e.g., "I have low self-esteem," "I'm not attractive enough," "I'm not smart enough," "I'm not good enough," "Everyone else is more successful than me."

Releasing unhelpful or limiting beliefs

Some of these limiting beliefs can stem from childhood, and even though they may have been well-intentioned, some have been passed down through the generations, and others could be harsh self-judgments that you've acquired along the way. The following steps will help you release the beliefs that are holding you back:

1. Identify: Recognizing limiting beliefs is the first step to transforming them. Now that you are aware of what form a limiting belief takes, you will find them easier to identify. Write down any beliefs you regularly think are holding you back. Whenever you feel stuck or discouraged, pause and ask yourself, "What belief about myself or the world is causing me to feel this way?"

2. Get evidence: Once you have identified your beliefs and written them down, the next step is to play the evidence game and ask yourself what actual evidence

supports this belief and what evidence contradicts it.

3. Question: Ask yourself whether the belief is something someone said to you. Was it a childhood experience? Or when did you decide it?

4. Get counter-evidence: Look for evidence of other people who have achieved this successfully or times in your life when you have broken this barrier.

5. Create a new story: Create a new and more empowering story that is realistic and optimistic. Write it down and refer to it multiple times a day, like an affirmation, to activate new neural networks.

For example:

The old belief: "I'm not creative."

The new story: "I can express my creativity in my own unique way."

6. Take action: Support the new story by taking small action steps and by telling yourself the new story daily so that it becomes a new belief.

The Evidence Game Example:

Belief: "I'm too old to start a new career."

Questioning: "Says who?"

"Society."

Counter-evidence: "Do I know anyone who's done this successfully?"

"Yes, I've read about people changing careers in their fifties or later."

Create a new story: "It's okay for me to explore a new venture and start a new career."

Take action: "I'm going to research training companies to get the skills I need and tell myself daily, "It's okay for me to explore a new venture and start a new career."

Release Ritual

You may also like to try this simple but powerful exercise:

- Write the limiting belief on a piece of paper.

- Close your eyes and imagine how your life will be different without this belief.

- Either safely burn the paper, or tear it up while saying, "I release this belief."

- Write your new, empowering belief on a fresh piece of paper.

- Keep this new belief somewhere visible for daily reinforcement.

You can also enlist the help of a hypnotherapist, Time Line Therapy® practitioner, or NLP practitioner to uncover and release multiple limiting beliefs.

Challenge Negative Self-Talk

Negative self-talk is one of the crucial elements that needs to be changed on the journey to becoming your authentic self. In Chapter Eight, we discussed turning negative what-if thinking around, using words of choice rather than words of pressure, and practicing self-compassion by using language that is both kind and positive.

In this chapter we have discussed limiting beliefs and how important it is to release them and create new beliefs that are empowering. By being mindful and paying attention to the language that you're using in your mind, then working with the techniques discussed earlier, you'll begin to make amazing changes in your life and empower your true self to shine.

Surround Yourself with Supportive, Encouraging People

Relationships play a crucial role in building self-esteem, but it's important to understand their proper place in your journey. Surrounding yourself with people who recognize and reflect your worth can be transformative. These individuals serve as mirrors, showing you aspects of yourself you might have overlooked or forgotten. However, true self-worth and self-esteem must ultimately come from within. External validation can support your growth, but it shouldn't be the foundation upon which your self-worth rests; it's important to learn to recognize and reinforce your own positive aspects and achievements (self-validation). On your journey to becoming your authentic self, it's beneficial to engage in activities where you can make new friends who see you for who you truly are or are becoming. Be open to letting go of any old friends who are not supportive of the real you or who you don't feel good around.

Discovering and Reinforcing Positive Aspects of Yourself

The journey of discovering and reinforcing positive aspects of yourself begins with understanding that you are multifaceted, comprised of both innate gifts and hard-earned wisdom. Just like a gemstone catching light from different angles, each facet of your personality reveals unique brilliance when given the chance to shine.

The process of self-discovery requires us to become curious observers of our own lives. Pay attention to the moments when you feel most alive, most genuine, and most in the flow. These instances are signposts pointing toward your authentic strengths. Perhaps you notice how time seems to dissolve when you're helping others work through their challenges or how you can naturally transform abstract concepts into clear, understandable ideas. Maybe you are great at organizing things. These are not coincidences; they're glimpses of your natural talents in action.

Compliments

The practice of accepting compliments deserves special attention on your journey of self-discovery. Many of us have been conditioned to deflect praise. However, it is important to accept and embrace the compliments that we are given. If somebody compliments you on your clothing and you say, "Oh, this old thing? I've had it for years," it's as if you are rejecting the compliment and saying that their opinion is not valid.

Initially, it can be uncomfortable to embrace compliments. However, it's a crucial part of accepting yourself and building your self-esteem. Imagine each compliment is a mirror reflecting a truth about yourself that others can see clearly. When somebody commends your creativity, resist the urge to discount it. Instead, take a moment to reflect on how your creative spirit has manifested in various aspects of your life.

Allow these observations from others to become windows through which you can view your capabilities more clearly. When someone gives you a compliment, respond with "Thank you," and own it by also saying, "It's my favorite too" or "I love it too," "That means a lot to me," "I love being creative," etc.

Imagine stepping into the compliment and "wearing" it. For example, how does it feel to be really confident? How does it feel to have creative talent? How does it feel to be wearing a beautiful shirt? Once you start to own your compliments, you begin creating opportunities for your strengths to flourish. For example, if you recognize your gift for bringing people together, you might find yourself naturally creating spaces for connection in your workplace or community. If you recognize your talent for putting amazing outfits together, you might find yourself starting a fashion blog.

I Am

When someone has low self-esteem or has been living inauthentically, it is often difficult to remember the good qualities or attributes they have as a person. What are five qualities or physical things you like about yourself?

Write them below:

1. _____

2. _____

3. _____

4. _____

5. _____

Sometimes, people struggle to even find five things that they like about themselves. If this is the case, I recommend this activity to help build your self-confidence and self-esteem.

Exercise:

> ➤ Draw a circle, then draw rays coming from it like the rays of the sun. Put your name or a picture of yourself in the center. On each of the rays, add one of the qualities or physical attributes that you like about yourself; add as many as you can possibly think of.

Qualities can be things like:

"I'm good at organizing."

"I'm kind."

"I'm generous."

"I'm intelligent."

"I'm loving."

Physical attributes can be things such as:

"I have nice teeth."

"I have lovely hair."

"I love my skin tone."

"I have a great butt."

"I have strong muscles."

Each evening before you go to sleep, read the things that you have written on the diagram out loud to yourself, e.g., "I am kind," "I have nice teeth," "I am generous," "I am loving," "I have lovely hair," etc. Whenever you think of something new that you like about yourself, add it to the diagram.

If you find yourself in a situation where someone is saying something negative about you, start to repeat the things you have written on the diagram to yourself quietly to negate what they are saying.

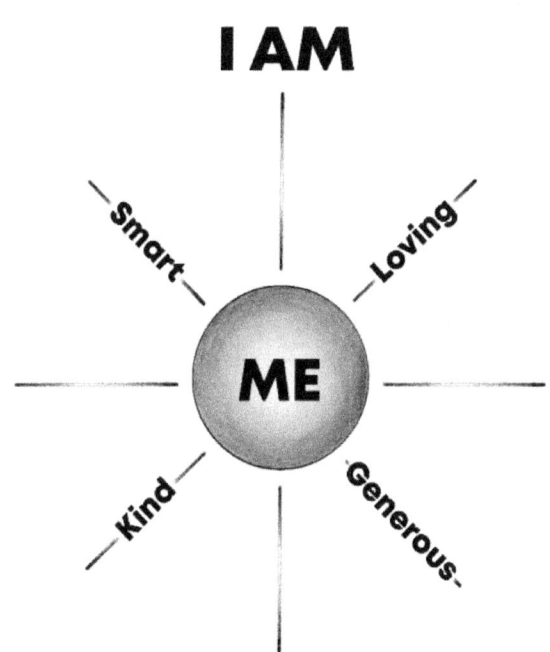

Keep a Journal to Document Your Successes and for Self-Reflection

One of the most effective tools in building self-esteem is maintaining a personal journal. This isn't merely about recording daily events or doing the exercises mentioned throughout this book; it's about creating a sacred space for self-reflection and celebration. Set aside time for quiet contemplation, and in these quiet moments of self-reflection, you will most likely discover that your greatest strengths have been there with you all along, waiting patiently to be recognized and embraced. Be sure to document your successes; it will help you to see just how far you have come.

Automatic writing can be a fun way to discover new things about yourself. Have a question in mind, e.g., "What am I really good at?" Sit quietly with a pen in your hand and allow words to flow freely onto the paper. This is about writing whatever comes without thinking about it. You may like to do it after a meditation or at a time when you're feeling relaxed. Automatic writing can help you to tap into your unconscious mind.

A Client Story

I'd like to share a story with you about one of my clients. Brandon, a forty-five-year-old financial analyst at a respected firm in Boston, appeared successful on the surface. With twenty years of professional experience and a comfortable six-figure salary, he projected competence at work. However, behind closed doors, his life told a different story. His marriage of fifteen years to Amy, a dominant personality who managed their household with ironclad control, had gradually eroded his sense of self-worth and autonomy.

At home, Brandon's opinions carried little weight. From decisions about their children's education to choices about household purchases, his input was often dismissed or criticized. He found himself walking on eggshells, second-guessing his every decision, and frequently apologizing for actions that didn't warrant remorse.

The constant criticism had seeped into his professional life, where he began hesitating to voice his ideas during meetings, despite his extensive experience and expertise.

The catalyst for change came during a family dinner when Amy berated Brandon in front of their children for purchasing the wrong brand of pasta sauce. As he watched his twelve-year-old daughter's face fall and his teenage son leave the table in embarrassment, Brandon realized that his passive acceptance of this treatment wasn't just affecting him—it was setting a devastating example for his children about relationships and self-worth.

Brandon scheduled an appointment with me. I helped him understand that his situation wasn't uncommon and that seeking help took courage and was the first step to regaining his life. Through our sessions, Brandon began to recognize patterns in his life that had contributed to his current situation.

He discovered that his tendency to give in to dominant personalities stemmed from his childhood experiences with a critical father. This awareness helped him understand why he had fallen into a similar pattern with Amy, unconsciously seeking approval through compliance. We also discovered the limiting beliefs that had been keeping him stuck, such as "I'm not good enough."

Brandon began taking steps to rebuild his self-esteem. He started with small, manageable steps that wouldn't immediately threaten the status quo but would help him establish a stronger sense of self. First, he created personal space by joining a local gym, dedicating two mornings a week to exercise before work. Prioritizing his health became his first act of independence. In this space, free from criticism, he began to reconnect with his body and his sense of capability.

At work, he started keeping a "Success Journal," documenting his daily achievements and positive interactions. This helped him recognize his professional competence, which he had begun to doubt as a result of his domestic situation. He sought out projects that showcased his expertise, gradually rebuilding his professional confidence.

At home, he created an "I am" chart to remember and reinforce his positive qualities and attributes. Whenever Amy was critical, he began running the "I am" statements through his mind to diminish her influence on his mood.

As Brandon's self-awareness grew, he worked on establishing healthy boundaries. He practiced simple assertiveness exercises, starting with small decisions at work and gradually extending to his home life. He learned to express his opinions calmly and firmly, using "I" statements to communicate his feelings and needs.

One significant breakthrough came when he calmly but firmly told Amy, "I feel disrespected when you criticize my decisions in front of the children. I need us to discuss our disagreements privately." Though met with initial resistance, this clear communication marked a turning point in their dynamic.

Brandon also focused on strengthening his support network beyond his marriage. He reconnected with old friends and joined a Men's Shed where he could connect and share experiences with other men. These connections provided perspective and reinforced that his feelings and needs were valid.

He began spending one-on-one time with his children, establishing relationships independent of their mother's influence. These interactions helped rebuild his confidence as a father and showed his children a different model of adult behavior.

The most challenging aspect of Brandon's journey was addressing the marital dynamic directly. After six months of working on himself and gaining confidence and self-esteem, he suggested couples counseling. Though Amy initially resisted, Brandon's newfound clarity about his needs and his willingness to consider alternatives if things didn't change led her to agree.

In couples therapy, they explored the roots of their dynamic, and Amy confronted her own controlling behavior, which stemmed from childhood insecurities. As Brandon became more assertive and emotionally stable, Amy began to see how her behavior had been pushing him away even though she actually desired his strength.

Over twelve months, Brandon underwent a remarkable transformation. His posture and body language shifted from apologetic to confident. Colleagues noticed and responded positively to his increased engagement in meetings and professional discussions. He received a promotion, partly due to his enhanced leadership presence.

At home, he began sharing equally in decision-making. While there were still conflicts, they were now handled with mutual respect rather than dominance and submission. He established regular "personal time" for hobbies and friendships, maintaining these boundaries even when met with resistance. Brandon also said that he finally felt present in his life rather than just going through the motions.

Most importantly, his relationship with his children was transformed. His son was proud of how his father had "become stronger," and his daughter began coming to him for advice, sensing his newfound emotional stability.

Brandon's journey from a henpecked husband to a confident, assertive individual demonstrates that with proper support, clarity of purpose, and consistent effort, it's possible to overcome deeply entrenched patterns of low self-esteem and reclaim your personal power, even in long-standing challenging relationships.

Chapter Ten

Resist Social Conditioning and Peer Pressure: Embrace Imperfection

"Your time is limited, so don't waste it living someone else's life. Don't be trapped by dogma - which is living with the results of other people's thinking. Don't let the noise of others' opinions drown out your own inner voice."

—Steve Jobs

In a world that constantly bombards us with expectations, definitions of success, and prescribed paths, finding and staying true to your authentic self is a profound journey of self-discovery. For some, the fear of rejection holds them back from breaking free of societal norms. However, the truth is that having the courage to follow your own path will bring more rewarding friendships and relationships with others. This chapter is an invitation to break free from the invisible chains of social conditioning and step into the most genuine version of yourself.

Questioning Societal Norms and Expectations

Most of us live our lives following a set of unwritten rules we never actually chose. From the moment you're born, there's an invisible playbook telling you exactly how life is "supposed" to look. *Go to school, get a good job, get married, have kids, buy a house, retire.*

This social programming comes from our families, educational institutions, media, and culture, and it weaves an intricate script about who we should be, how we should look, what we should want, and how we should live, love, work, and exist. But what if that script doesn't actually fit your life?

These expectations are often so deeply ingrained that we mistake them for personal choices and questioning them is crucial to discovering your true self. Take a moment and think about the expectations you've accepted without question:

- Career paths predetermined by family or culture.

- Relationship structures that don't resonate with your true self.

- Your worth is determined by how much money you make or how you look.

- Happiness means following a specific life path.

- Beauty standards that erase diversity, and individual uniqueness.

- Success means having a fancy job title, material goods, and/or a large bank balance.

Start paying attention to the "shoulds" in your life.

"I should get married by thirty."

"I should have a certain type of career."

"I should have kids by now."

"I should look a certain way."

Every time you hear yourself thinking or saying "should," it's a red flag. It means you're following someone else's script rather than writing your own. It's important to start getting curious about the norms you have accepted. Ask yourself the following questions:

"Who decided this was the right way to live?"

"Does this truly align with my core values, or am I simply performing a role designed by others?" (i.e., parents, social media, friends, society)

"Whose standards am I trying to meet?"

"Who benefits from me conforming to these expectations?"

Challenge the stories you've been told about success and happiness. Success isn't one size fits all. For some people, success is climbing the corporate ladder. For others, it's creating art, traveling the world, or raising a family. There's no universal definition—except the one you create for yourself.

Notice how media and advertising shape your expectations. Companies make money by making you feel like you're not enough. They create problems you didn't know you had, then sell you solutions. That perfect life you see on Instagram? It's a carefully curated marketing strategy, not real life.

Get comfortable with being uncomfortable. Questioning societal norms doesn't mean rejecting everything. It means creating space for discernment. Some societal norms have merit, while others are outdated.

Begin to choose the things that feel right or preferable to you. It might mean a career path that excites you, not just one that looks good on paper. Maybe it's getting a tattoo because you love body art, even if your family and friends don't, not as an act of rebellion or to follow the masses but as a genuine personal choice. Maybe it's simply allowing yourself to want something different.

Questioning the norms isn't about being different for the sake of being different. It's about being true to yourself. It's about consciously creating a life that feels authentic not just acceptable, and choosing which societal constructs serve your growth and which limit your potential. Doing what's right for you might feel like you're going against the grain. Your family might not understand. Your friends might think you're weird, but living someone else's life is much more uncomfortable in the long run.

Seeking Diverse Perspectives and Experiences

To truly understand yourself, it's good to expose yourself to diverse perspectives and experiences. If you stay in your comfort zone, you risk becoming a prisoner of your own limited perspective, and your full potential is not explored. By intentionally seeking out different viewpoints, cultures, and ways of living, you expand your understanding of what's possible.

Travel, if you can, or watch documentaries about different cultures and places or alternative lifestyles. Read books by authors with radically different life experiences. Engage with people whose backgrounds are different from yours. Attend cultural events, workshops, and gatherings outside your comfort zone, listen to stories that challenge your existing narratives and practice listening with no judgment. Each new perspective is a window into understanding not just the world, but yourself. By exploring diversity, you will discover parts of yourself you didn't know existed and might never have uncovered within your immediate environment. Exposure to diverse perspectives creates new neural pathways. You're not just collecting information; you're rewiring your brain's interpretative mechanisms and opening yourself to a whole new world.

Developing a Strong Sense of Self Separate from Group Identity

Developing a sense of self, separate from group identity, is perhaps the most challenging aspect of this journey. We are social creatures, hardwired to seek belonging. But true authenticity requires the courage to distinguish between collective identity and individual essence. This doesn't mean rejecting community but rather creating a self that can exist both within and beyond group narratives.

The first step to having a strong sense of self begins with self-awareness. Many of us unconsciously absorb identities like protective camouflage—professional titles, cultural backgrounds, family roles, religious affiliations, and social group memberships become so intertwined with our sense of self that we struggle to distinguish where these external identities end and our true self begins.

This process is about understanding who you are beyond those external identities. Ask yourself "who am I when nobody is watching?" "What do I personally like and enjoy?"

Everything we have covered in this book so far is helping you to reach the point where you can stand strong in your own sense of self, in your own power. In Chapter Six, we explored personal values, discovering what drives you and then learning to differentiate between external expectations and your internal desires. Respect your values by setting and enforcing boundaries. Practice saying no without guilt. Being able to say "No" to plans, expectations, and roles that don't fit is how you create space for your true self.

Begin to trust your own voice by developing the courage to make choices that feel right to you, even when they don't make sense to anyone else. Your family might not understand why you're changing; your friends might think you're going through a phase. But this isn't about them—it's about you discovering who you really are.

Emotional independence is a skill that develops as you begin to validate your own experiences, trust your intuition, and make decisions based on your internal compass rather than relying on external validation. Cultivating a positive inner dialogue is another tool that helps you to withstand external pressures from peers. In Chapter Five and Chapter Eight, you learned the tools to change your inner voice and be kinder to yourself, using positive language and turning negative what-if thoughts around. By reinforcing to yourself that the decisions and choices you are making are right for you, that you have a right to do what is best for you, and that it's okay to be you even if others do things differently, you are boosting your self-reliance.

Journaling is a powerful tool in the process of building your own identity rather than doing what everyone else does. Write about your dreams, your fears, your secret hopes. Use your journal to write down the things that you enjoy doing and the people you feel good around and also the things and people that diminish your sense of self, your confidence, or your happiness. All the journaling, referred to in previous chapters, which you have started doing, is already helping you define who you are and what you stand for.

Trying new experiences without worrying about what others will think and placing yourself in environments where your usual group identities don't define you will help you to gain confidence in being yourself. When you understand the difference between belonging and conformity, it becomes clear that being authentic is more important than being a follower. Belonging is about being accepted for your authentic self; conformity is about changing yourself to be accepted. True belonging allows for individuality, while conformity demands uniformity. Choose relationships and communities that celebrate your unique essence rather than requiring you to hide or dim your light and recognize that your worth is not determined by how well you fit into a group's expectations but by your commitment to personal integrity. Your story is not predetermined by your family, friends, culture, or professional background—it's a living, evolving creation, and you are the author.

The ultimate goal is not to reject group identities entirely but to engage with them consciously. You can appreciate your cultural heritage, professional community, or family traditions without being confined by them. The difference is choice—you choose how much of these identities to integrate rather than being unconsciously defined by them.

Your true self as an individual is something you create, day by day, choice by choice, with courage, compassion, and an unwavering commitment to your own truth, and when you honor your truth, nothing and no one will be able to sway you from it.

Letting Go of Unrealistic Standards

Unrealistic standards are psychological traps that prevent you from experiencing genuine self-acceptance and happiness.

Unrealistic standards often stem from:

- Comparing yourself to curated social media personas.

- Criticisms or expectations that you internalized during childhood.

- Cultural and professional benchmarks that rarely account for individual complexity.

Our culture bombards us with impossible standards and restrictive definitions of success. These standards are judgments related to our physical body, our mental aptitude, our ability to earn money, to perform at a sport, to achieve the elements of a "perfect life," a "perfect relationship," etc. And they suffocate personal growth and authentic expression. Letting go of these standards is an act of absolute self-love. It means recognizing that your self-worth is not determined by external achievements but by the integrity of your inner life.

Take an inventory of which standards you are trying to live up to and ask yourself if behaving in this way is bringing you closer to your true self or requires you to act in a way that causes you stress and unhappiness. When you begin to develop a compassionate relationship with yourself and acknowledge that being a human is messy, challenging, and deeply personal, you will start to enjoy the freedom of being you.

Finding Beauty in Your Unique Quirks and Flaws

Perfection is a myth that holds you in an ongoing state of inadequacy. Your imperfections are not errors that need to be corrected but signatures of your unique self. They are treasures to be celebrated and the brushstrokes that make your life's canvas distinctive. Everybody has some quirks or imperfections; some people have one foot larger than the other, some require corrective lenses to read or see distance, many women have one breast larger than the other, ears may be asymmetrical, scars and birthmarks are common, and the list goes on....

When you embrace your imperfections, learning to love and accept yourself as you are, you disarm the critical voices, both external and internal. Your scars, your struggles, your unconventional dreams—these are not flaws to be hidden but beautiful markers of your unique journey. Every scar tells a story of survival, every quirk represents your distinct personality, and every unconventional choice is a testament to your individual spirit. Once you begin making choices to love and accept yourself, you will find it easier to reject things your peers are doing that don't resonate with you, whereas previously you may have complied to "keep the peace" or to "belong."

Your journey is not about becoming someone else's version of perfect but about becoming unabashedly, radiantly you.

Celebrate Progress Over Perfection

Becoming your authentic self and maintaining it is a continual work in progress. Each small step, each moment of courage, each instance of choosing yourself is a victory worth acknowledging. Progress, not perfection, is the mantra of authentic living. Many people get stuck in the cycle of needing to be perfect before they will do something or go somewhere, such

143

as publishing a book, selling their artwork or handmade creations, speaking in public, applying for a job, going to an event, or starting a business. If you wait until the book is perfect, you will never publish it; if you wait until you're fully comfortable speaking in public, you will never do it; if you need to look or be perfect before you embrace the dating scene, you will hold yourself back from true connection.

Needing to be perfect in any area of your life will keep you trapped in what is rather than what could be. Perhaps there's a fear of failure holding you back, but in reality, there is no failure; it's simply feedback telling you that it can be done differently next time. Celebrate the small moments where you choose yourself— where you set a boundary, pursue a passion, or simply stand in your truth without apology. Celebrating your progress has been referred to throughout this book as it is a step that many people overlook. Acknowledging how far you have come and celebrating your progress will enable you to keep the momentum going.

Surround Yourself with Authentic, Supportive Individuals

The company you keep is an important factor in your well-being and ability to stay true to yourself. Toxic relationships and unsupportive networks can erode your sense of self. Take a look at your current relationships, and if necessary, create boundaries that protect your authentic self. Develop discernment in connections with others. Authenticity requires a supportive network—people who see your potential, challenge you constructively, respect your boundaries, and create space for your growth. Look for friends or partners who celebrate your uniqueness rather than try to mold you into their expectations. These are the relationships that become mirrors, reflecting your truest self back to you.

Finding communities aligned with your values becomes an essential part of this process. Look for groups that encourage individual expression, encourage personal growth, challenge you intellectually and emotionally, and recognize the unique contribution only you can make. These are the people that become "your tribe" I lived in Hawaii for many years, and the term "ohana" is used for family. However, this does not just mean your blood relatives. It also encompasses your chosen family of friends and people who support you. I think we all need to find our ohana and embrace these connections that nourish and nurture our soul.

Mentorship

Engaging a mentor can be a wonderful way to have support and motivation to keep moving forward on your journey. Mentorship is not about becoming a carbon copy of someone else. It's about learning from individuals who embody qualities that you respect. These aren't necessarily people from similar backgrounds or cultures or who have identical life experiences, but individuals who have maintained integrity to their core values despite external pressures. A true mentor is someone who inspires you to explore your own path. They will help you recognize and acknowledge the progress you are making, which in turn assists you to move through challenging times or times when you may feel stuck.

Look for someone who demonstrates integrity, has navigated challenges with grace, shows vulnerability, maintains authenticity across multiple areas of their life and prioritizes personal growth. When you find the person who has the qualities you admire and respect, ask them if they are open to being a mentor for you. This may be in the capacity of a life coach or business coach that you hire, or simply someone that you ask to mentor you.

Priya's Story

Priya was working on her laptop in a bustling downtown Seattle coffee shop when she made the decision to email me. At twenty-five, she was overwhelmed by trying to navigate a different kind of cultural landscape—one that seemed simultaneously more open and more challenging than the world she'd left behind in Mumbai.

Moving to the United States for her master's in technology had been more than an academic decision. It was an escape, an exploration, and a profound act of self-discovery. Her family had initially supported the move, seeing it as a prestigious opportunity. What they didn't realize was how deeply this journey would transform her understanding of herself.

The first eighteen months were a whirlwind of adaptation. Coming from a traditional Maharashtrian family, Priya had arrived with a lifetime of internalized expectations—good girl, dutiful daughter, and future wife. But Seattle—with its progressive culture, diverse communities, and unapologetic individualism—

147

began to crack open those carefully constructed narratives.

Her graduate program in tech was her first experience of professional environments where women were not just present but leaders. She joined women in tech groups, attended conferences, and slowly began to dismantle the subtle conditioning that had told her to be less visible, less ambitious.

The diversity in Seattle introduced her to people from countless backgrounds—LGBTQ+ colleagues, first-generation immigrants, activists, and artists. Every interaction expanded her understanding of identity and challenged the narrow definitions she'd grown up with.

Culture shock came in unexpected moments. The directness of American communication contrasted sharply with the indirect, harmony-preserving communication style of her childhood. During our sessions, Priya started learning how to communicate assertively and how to put boundaries in place. She learned to speak up, to disagree, and to advocate for herself—skills that felt both terrifying and liberating to her.

Her family's expectations loomed large, even from thousands of miles away. Weekly video calls were a delicate dance of revelation and omission. They didn't know about her growing independence, her questioning of traditional marriage structures, and her exploration of relationships outside their expected framework.

Together, Priya and I unpacked the layers of her cultural conditioning and discovered how her sense of self had been shaped by familial and societal expectations. Priya did lots of journaling, which helped her uncover more of who she was and what she really wanted in her life. We explored how she could construct an identity that was authentically her own and used hypnotherapy to help her build confidence in herself.

Priya was offered work in a cutting-edge tech startup, and it became more than just a job; it was a space of personal transformation. She discovered her voice in team meetings, challenged project approaches, and became known for her innovative thinking. The professional world was teaching her that her worth wasn't about being agreeable but about being authentic and creative.

Cultural identity became fluid as she learned to embrace the combination of being Indian and increasingly American. Some days this meant wearing a sari to work. Other days it meant leading a technology workshop in jeans and a graphic tee. She stopped seeing these as contradictions and started viewing them as different expressions of her multifaceted self.

Dating added another layer of complexity as she navigated relationships outside the arranged marriage model that her family expected. Priya learned about being comfortable with the way she looked, about consent, mutual respect, and partnership in ways that were entirely new to her. Each relationship taught her more about understanding herself, her boundaries, and her desires.

We discussed looking for a supportive community, and Priya found a network of first-generation immigrants, women of color in tech, and progressive South Asian communities. These weren't just social groups of like-minded people; they were support systems that understood the intricate process of cultural navigation and self-discovery. One of the women Priya met at a group became her mentor, having been through a similar journey when she arrived in the USA ten years previously.

Eventually, her parents' perspective began to shift. Not immediately and not without tension but gradually. As they saw her success, her happiness, and her growing sense of self, their role became less about control and more about understanding.

Priya embraced her new self fully. No longer defined by cultural expectations, family pressures, or societal norms, she was entirely her own person, loving herself and her new life.

Chapter Eleven

The Rebuilding of Self: Navigating with COMPASS

"Embrace your uniqueness, live life, and love yourself unapologetically."

—Carolyn G.A Ching

ongratulations on making it this far! Let's take a look at how to put together everything you've learned so far. The first step is simple yet profound: it's developing self-awareness, and that means paying attention to yourself. The fact that you've read the book to this point means you will certainly have taken the first step and have already gained more awareness about yourself and what it is you need to change. Use each chapter as a resource and begin making changes one step at a time. Real change is a work in progress... Some days you'll nail it, and some days you may struggle—and that's completely okay. Persevere! It is worth it! You may like to use the affirmation: "Every day I am learning, growing, and becoming more authentically me."

I have divided each of the client stories in this chapter under the headings of the COMPASS framework so that you can see the various challenges people experienced and what they subsequently worked on to become authentic.

Marco's Journey: The Mechanic's Roadmap to Personal Transformation

Before COMPASS

The Garage of Life

Marco stood in his garage, surrounded by tools that had become extensions of his hands, reflecting on a journey far more complex than any engine repair. His life seemed to revolve around work, making money as quickly as possible, and then isolating himself at home with his dog, too exhausted to socialize. He really wanted a partner but realized he didn't even know who he was, let alone what he wanted in a partner.

The COMPASS Transformation

Taming the Comparison Monster

As a young mechanic, Marco began the destructive habit of constantly measuring himself against others—his colleagues' faster repairs, their seemingly more successful careers, their ease with dating girls. Over time, his self-worth and confidence were eroded like rust on the cars he repaired.

Marco learned that true growth wasn't about competing but about personal progression. It wasn't about dating a different girl every month but about loving himself and having the courage to be authentic, to attract a partner for more than superficial looks. He started tracking his improvements, celebrating his unique skills, and practicing gratitude rather than looking at his perceived areas of lack.

Breaking the Overthinking Cycle

Overthinking paralyzed Marco like a seized engine. He'd spend hours ruminating on potential problems, imagining worst-case scenarios for every repair, every date he wanted to go on but backed out of, and every life

155

decision. This mental gridlock prevented action and innovation.

Learning to manage his thoughts became crucial. He developed strategies: setting time limits for problem-solving, using the 5-5-5 method, turning his what-if thinking around, and recognizing when analysis was transforming into paralysis. He learned to trust himself and the decisions he made and stopped trying to control outcomes.

Realigning Misaligned Values

Marco realized his life had been running off course. He'd been pursuing external markers of success—more jobs, faster earnings—without considering his deeper values of craftsmanship, integrity, service to others, and personal growth.

He began realigning, prioritizing quality over quantity, valuing relationships over transactions, and ensuring his daily actions reflected his core beliefs. His work became not just about fixing machines but about serving people and maintaining professional integrity.

Overcoming People Pleasing and Communicating Assertively

Prior to our sessions, Marco was the mechanic who always said "Yes"—accepting every job, working overtime, and pandering to his employees. He worked most weekends and hadn't taken a vacation in five years. He was afraid of disappointing others, sacrificing his own well-being instead.

Gradually, he learned to set boundaries. He started communicating clearly with clients about realistic timelines, fair pricing, and the scope of repairs. He set boundaries with his employees regarding hours of work, pay, and diligence. He discovered that assertiveness wasn't aggression—it was self-respect in action. He began closing the garage on Saturday afternoons and Sundays and also scheduled vacation time in his planner.

Eliminating Avoidance and Embracing Vulnerability

Avoidance had been Marco's default mechanism for handling challenges—both at work and in his personal life. He always found ways to sidestep difficult conversations, personal vulnerabilities, or challenging repairs.

Becoming truly authentic, he learned, meant facing discomfort head-on. He started accepting challenging repair jobs that pushed his skills, practicing assertive communication, having difficult conversations with family and colleagues, and sharing his journey of personal growth. He also challenged himself to smile and talk to women when he was standing in line at the bank or grocery store rather than always looking away.

Combating Self-Doubt and Building Self-Esteem

Years of self-doubt and comparing himself to others had eroded Marco's confidence. He'd question every diagnosis, every repair, every life decision. He didn't date because he figured no one would want to go out with him, and he never had time anyway.

Building self-esteem became a deliberate practice. We released some unhelpful beliefs around success, attractiveness, and worthiness. Marco started noting his successes in a journal no matter how small. Each successfully repaired vehicle became a testament to his skill and every decision he made that turned out well was documented. He decided to go on a blind date his friend set up for him and was surprised to find he enjoyed himself. He learned to separate his self-worth from external validation and rely on his own measures of progress instead.

Resisting Social Conditioning and Embracing Imperfection

Society had told Marco what success should look like—a busy garage, expensive equipment, employees, a great reputation, and a healthy bank balance. But he realized true success was about authenticity, continuous learning, and embracing imperfections.

The Outcome

Marco learned that personal growth is about understanding, adapting, and moving forward. The changes he made led him to feel more fulfilled in his work life, he gained a reputation for good quality work at a fair price and as his confidence in himself grew, he began dating someone who appreciated him for being himself.

Leilani's Journey: Finding Her True Self in the Classroom

Before COMPASS

The Burned-Out People Pleaser

Leilani had always wanted to be a kindergarten teacher. She appeared to be the perfect teacher, always smiling, always prepared, and always going above and beyond. But inside was a different reality. Her days were an exhausting performance of constant people pleasing. She volunteered for every school committee, stayed late designing elaborate classroom decorations, and spent her weekends creating personalized learning materials. She organized fundraisers to supply basic supplies for children in her community. Her fellow teachers admired her, and parents praised her, but Leilani was frustrated and emotionally exhausted.

The COMPASS Transformation

Taming the Comparison Monster

Leilani realized she was constantly measuring herself against the seemingly perfect teachers on social media. Elaborate classroom displays, matching outfits, seemingly endless energy— she felt perpetually inadequate. The first major step on her journey to change was to stop her frequent scrolling of social media.

Breaking the Overthinking Cycle

Nights were spent obsessively planning, replanning, and second-guessing every lesson and interaction. Leilani learned to set boundaries with her own thoughts. She began to:

- Limit planning time to specific hours.

- Practice mindfulness to stay present.

- Use the 5-5-5 method to combat ruminating.

- Trust her professional instincts.

Realigning Misaligned Values

Leilani discovered her core values were being overshadowed by expectations. When she elicited her values, it became clear that she wanted to:

- Prioritize children's emotional learning.

- Create a nurturing, fun, and inclusive environment.

- Maintain her mental health.

161

- Have a life outside teaching (work-life balance).

She began redesigning her approach, focusing on fulfilling her values rather than creating perfect presentations and trying to be the perfect teacher.

Overcoming People Pleasing

This was her biggest challenge. Leilani learned to:

- Say "No" to extra committees.

- Set clear boundaries with demanding parents.

- Communicate her needs to school administration using "I" statements.

- Recognize that her worth wasn't determined by being constantly available.

Eliminating Avoidance and Embracing Vulnerability

Instead of hiding her frustrations and struggles, Leilani started sharing her challenges with trusted colleagues and being honest about her burnout. She found an online teacher support group, which she started attending. Leilani also learned to ask for help when she needed it, rather than doing everything herself.

Combating Self-Doubt and Building Self-Esteem

Leilani started keeping a success journal and made a note every time she successfully said "No" to something. She started writing down compliments from parents and putting the pieces of paper in a jar. On days when she was tempted to doubt herself, she read through the compliments and began to feel more confident. By doing this, she began to understand that perfection is impossible, but the impact she was having on her students by being real was immeasurable.

Resisting Social Conditioning

Leilani challenged the stereotype of the martyr-teacher. She rejected the idea that good teachers sacrifice everything and she prioritized self-care as a professional necessity. Her online support group helped her realize that the simple things related to her culture that she enjoyed bringing into the classroom were more valuable than the time-consuming displays she had previously struggled to produce. Over time, she created a sustainable work-life balance and defined success by noting the happiness of the children in her class, not by her own exhaustion.

The Outcome

Within a year, Leilani's classroom was transformed. She was more relaxed, her students were happier and more engaged, and she had rediscovered her passion for teaching. Her breakthrough came when she started focusing on her unique strengths. She recognized her genuine gift wasn't in creating the most Instagram-worthy classroom or providing everything for her students but in her ability to truly connect with children, to see and nurture their individual spirits.

Leilani said, "I'm not here to be a perfect teacher. I'm here to be a present, authentic teacher who helps children love learning and understand their own worth." And she told me that the most important lesson she learned is that "You can't pour from an empty cup."

Juan's Journey: Redefining Strength from the Inside Out

Before COMPASS

The Muscle-Bound Façade

Juan Martinez looked the epitome of masculine fitness. At 32, he was a top personal trainer with a body seemingly carved of granite, a huge social media following, and a reputation for pushing clients to their absolute limits. But behind the chiseled abs and motivational posts, Juan was drowning in a sea of unresolved emotions and impossible expectations and found himself becoming increasingly aggressive with the people around him. From the outside, he was a success story. Muscular, successful, and always confident. Inside, he was a pressure cooker of unexpressed feelings, toxic masculinity, and deep-seated insecurities.

The COMPASS Transformation

Taming the Comparison Monster

Juan's entire identity was built on comparison. He constantly measured himself against other fitness influencers, athletes, and clients. Every workout, every client's transformation, and every social media post became a competition.

His breakthrough came when he realized true strength wasn't about being better than others but about being better than his previous self. He stopped scrolling through social media and feeling inadequate, and he started tracking his personal growth instead of looking for external validation.

Breaking the Overthinking Cycle

Years of mental battles had turned his mind into a relentless cycle of negativity:

- Constant performance anxiety

- Obsessive workout planning

- Paralyzing fear of not being "enough"

During our sessions, Juan learned meditation, journaling, and rewiring of his negative thoughts. He began to implement boundaries, practice mindfulness, and distinguish between productive reflection and destructive rumination.

Realigning Misaligned Values

Fitness had always been Juan's shield—a way to prove his worth, to hide his vulnerabilities. He discovered that his true values went far beyond physical strength: genuine human connection, holistic wellness, being able to help others, and authentic leadership were all important to him.

Once he became aware of his values, he redesigned his training approach from pure physical transformation to holistic life coaching where he could develop deeper connections with clients and help them in multiple areas of their lives.

Overcoming People Pleasing

As a trainer, Juan had built a persona of the "tough guy" who never said "No." He would take on every client, work endless hours, suppress his own needs, and never show weakness.

Learning to set boundaries became crucial. He started being honest about his capacity: saying "No" to clients and opportunities that didn't align with his values, communicating his needs clearly, and recognizing the importance of time for himself.

Eliminating Avoidance and Embracing Vulnerability

The biggest challenge was emotional openness. Juan had spent years avoiding difficult conversations and emotions. He began exploring his emotions in therapy and joined a supportive men's group. He shared his struggles with trusted friends and started teaching his clients that mental fitness is as important as physical fitness.

Combating Self-Doubt and Building Self-Esteem

Juan's self-worth had always been tied to his physical appearance and performance, so he began exploring and ultimately changing the beliefs he had about appearance, masculinity, and success. He started to celebrate nonphysical achievements and understand that his worth had nothing to do with muscle mass. Through journaling he discovered that strength includes emotional resilience.

Resisting Social Conditioning

Juan challenged toxic masculinity head-on. He:

- Rejected the "never show weakness" narrative.

- Embraced emotional intelligence.

- Redefined strength as comprehensive wellness.

- Became a role model for authentic masculinity.

The Outcome

Juan's business and personal life transformed. He became calmer and more content. He qualified as a meditation teacher. He lost some of his old clients and experienced some negative comments on social media as he moved into holistic coaching. However, he gained a deeply committed community. His training approach now focused on:

- Holistic wellness

- Mental health

- Emotional intelligence

- Personal growth

- Fitness for health

Juan's new training philosophy is "Real strength isn't about how much you can lift. It's about how honestly you can live, how deeply you can connect, and how courageously you can grow." He invited me to pass on a note to everyone fighting their inner battles: "Your journey is valid, your growth matters, prioritize you!"

Kirsty's Journey: Breaking Free and Finding Herself

Before COMPASS

Drowning in Disapproval

The morning sunlight caught the small silver pendant around Kirsty's neck—a gift to herself, marking one year of freedom. It wasn't an expensive piece of jewelry, but it represented something far more precious: her reclaimed life.

Seven years with Jason had been like living inside a gradually tightening vise. When they first met, he was magnetic—the kind of man who could walk into a room and command everyone's attention. Kirsty had been drawn to his confidence, mistaking his intensity for passion and his control for love.

It started subtly. A comment about her outfit. A raised eyebrow at her career choices. Disapproval of her friends. Gentle corrections that initially felt like guidance. By the time she realized she was drowning, the water had risen past her mouth, nearly to her eyes.

Her transformation didn't happen overnight. It was a series of small rebellions, of reclaiming herself piece by piece.

The COMPASS Transformation

Taming the Comparison Monster

The first breakthrough came through therapy. Kirsty learned about the comparison trap she'd fallen into, constantly measuring herself against the impossible standards Jason had created—other women, other versions of herself, imaginary perfections that existed only in his critical gaze. I helped her understand that comparison was a losing game, especially when the referee was someone who didn't want her to win and constantly shifted the goalposts.

Breaking the Overthinking Cycle

Overthinking had been her constant companion. Every conversation with Jason became a mental chess game, anticipating his moves and trying to prevent his anger. Her mind was a battlefield of endless scenarios, what-ifs, and silent apologies.

Meditation became her first real weapon of defense—a way to quiet the storm inside her head and start listening to her own voice. Kirsty also learned to change the negative thoughts and what-if thoughts she was constantly contemplating.

Realigning Misaligned Values

Kirsty's values had become so tangled with Jason's expectations that she'd forgotten who she was. Nursing—her true passion—had been reduced to something he deemed acceptable, something small enough not to threaten his sense of control. He conceded that she could enroll in a short course to become a certified clinical medical assistant, and slowly she began to untangle herself.

Overcoming People Pleasing

People pleasing had been her survival mechanism. Kirsty had become an expert at reading Jason's moods, at becoming exactly what he wanted. Learning to say "No" was like learning a foreign language—awkward at first, then liberating. While she was still living in the same house, she had to choose carefully which things she said "No" to, as her personal safety was most important. Each small boundary was an act of courage.

Eliminating Avoidance and Embracing Vulnerability

Vulnerability had always terrified Kirsty. Jason had taught her that showing emotion was weakness and that her feelings were inconvenient. She joined a yoga class, which became her sanctuary. As she began to trust a new friend, she discovered that sharing small pieces of her story wasn't a confession of failure but an act of incredible strength.

Combating Self-Doubt and Building Self-Esteem

Self-doubt had been Jason's most effective weapon. He knew how to plant seeds of uncertainty to make Kirsty question her perception of reality. To make her believe she was worthless and wouldn't make it on her own. We worked on changing some limiting beliefs and building her self-confidence. Rebuilding her self-esteem was a daily practice. She started small—celebrating her professional achievements, celebrating her progress in yoga, making new friends, acknowledging her resilience, and speaking kindly to herself.

Resisting Social Conditioning

Breaking free from social conditioning was perhaps her greatest challenge. She lived in a small town, and society had countless unspoken rules about relationships, about what women should tolerate, and about the shame of leaving. Kirsty was rewriting those rules, one day at a time. She also learned to accept that the flaws and quirks Jason had highlighted and criticized in her were simply normal, natural, beautiful parts of herself.

The Outcome

A year after leaving Jason, Kirsty was different. Not hardened but stronger. Not bitter but wiser. She was flourishing at work and looking into studying nursing in the future. Her relationships with friends were genuine, and she had slowly reconnected with her family and some of her old friends. She was regaining her confidence in all aspects of her life. The pendant around her neck wasn't just a symbol of her past—it was a promise to herself to keep moving forward and to maintain her true self at all times. Her journey wasn't about revenge or proving Jason wrong. It was about proving to herself that she was worthy of respect, of love, of living her life fully on her own terms.

Kirsty shared, "I am not defined by my past relationship but by how I choose to heal, grow, and love myself."

See resources for support.[1]

These stories demonstrate that continuous self-reflection is important, as is the commitment to change, along with the courage to be vulnerable and acceptance that everyone's journey is different. The people in these stories would all tell you, "If I can do it, you can too!"

---

[1] Resources for support in USA:
National Domestic Violence Hotline: 1-800-799-7233
RAINN National Sexual Assault Hotline: 1-800-656-4673
In Australia:
National Domestic Violence/Sexual Assault Hotline: 1800 737 73

Chapter Twelve

Living and Loving Your Authentic Life

"To be yourself in a world that is constantly trying to make you something else is the greatest accomplishment."

—Ralph Waldo Emerson

As we reach the final chapter of our journey together, it's time to celebrate the transformation you've undertaken. Throughout this book, we've explored the COMPASS framework—a roadmap to rediscovering and embracing your most authentic self—which, in turn, allows you to uncover your true passion and purpose. Now, it's about turning those insights into a living reality.

Authenticity is a daily practice, and each day presents new opportunities to:

- Choose yourself over external expectations.

- Listen to your inner voice.

- Stand firm in your values.

- Embrace vulnerability.

- Grow and change.

Practical Daily Practices

A great way to sustain your authentic life is to integrate these practices into your daily routine:

Morning Reflection (20–30 mins)

Allow some extra time in the morning in a quiet, uninterrupted space and start each day with a self-check-in. Ask yourself:

➢ How am I truly feeling right now, beneath the surface?

➢ What internal voices am I hearing today?

Remind yourself of who you really are and what matters to you.

Each morning brings a fresh opportunity to realign with your truest self, peel back the layers of expectation, and reconnect with your inner wisdom.

➤ Write down two authentic intentions for your day in connection with:

- Setting or maintaining a personal boundary.

- Owning your mistakes.

- Compassionate self-talk.

- Speaking your truth kindly and respectfully.

- Standing up for what you believe in.

- Making decisions based on your values.

- Resisting pressure to conform, knowing it's okay to be different.

Navigating the Day

As you move through your day, authenticity becomes a living, breathing practice. When faced with moments that challenge your truth—whether in workplace interactions, social gatherings, or personal relationships—pause. Take a breath. Remember that your worth is not determined by others' expectations or approval.

When people-pleasing temptations arise, notice the physical signals. Does your body become tense? Does your breath become shallow? These are invitations to reconnect with your core. Allow yourself to pause before responding; "Let me think about that and get back to you" is a powerful statement of self-respect. Your truth can be calm, clear, and kind.

The comparison monster will try to seduce you—through social media, workplace dynamics, or social gatherings. When it whispers that you're not enough, recognize this is just an old, familiar story. Redirect your focus. Your journey is uniquely yours, and comparison is the thief of authenticity. You are choosing a different path.

Self-doubt may visit. When it does, acknowledge it. Authenticity isn't about being fearless; it's about moving forward despite fear. You might wonder if being your true self is worth it. Trust the process—it gets easier and more rewarding over time. Write down your achievements as a record of your growth. Every challenge overcome, every moment of vulnerability, is a testament to your strength.

Be consistent: Aim to be the same person at work, at home, and with friends.

Keep promises made to yourself: If you say you'll do something for yourself, do it; treat promises to yourself as seriously as promises to others.

Fear of conflict may arise. Being true to yourself might lead to disagreements. That's okay—respectful disagreement is healthy.

Old habits might suck you in, and you may slip into old ways of acting. Don't worry; just gently remind yourself to be authentic. Before acting, take a deep breath and ask, "Is this aligned with my true self?"

In our hyper-connected world, authenticity requires intentional digital boundaries. Follow social media accounts that inspire growth, not comparison. Use technology as a tool for connection and learning, not as a measure of your worth.

When you face moments of doubt, societal pressure, and internal resistance, simply acknowledge your feelings without judgment, return to the COMPASS principles, reconnect with your core values, seek support from trusted allies, and remember how far you've already come.

Evening Reflection and Recalibration (15–20 mins)

Each evening create a sacred space for reflection. This isn't about judgment but understanding. Review your day with a gentle heart:

> ➤ What moments felt truly "me" today?

> ➤ Where did I momentarily disconnect from myself?

> ➤ Did I honor my true self today?

> ➤ What learnings can I take from today's experiences?

This simple act of reflection can realign you with your core values and intentions. There are no wrong answers, only opportunities for deeper self-understanding.

The Weekly Reset

Once a week, typically on a Sunday evening, create a ritual of review and renewal. You may like to write a compassionate letter to yourself. Recognize your efforts and your humanity and forgive yourself for the moments where you didn't show up for yourself. Celebrate your moments of genuine living and identify areas of growth to focus on for the coming week.

Emergency Authenticity Tool Kit

When overwhelm threatens, return to basics. Breathe deeply. Take a short walk in nature or step outside and feel the earth beneath your feet. Do a 5-minute meditation and use positive, empowering self-talk. Ask yourself, "What would my most authentic self need right now?" Sometimes, it's rest. Sometimes, it's action. Always, it's compassion.

The Ripple Effect of Authenticity

Your journey of authenticity doesn't just transform you—it has a ripple effect and inspires others. By being your true self, you:

- Permit those around you to do the same.

- Challenge restrictive social norms.

- Create spaces of genuine connection.

- Contribute to a more empathetic, understanding world.

In Chapter Two, I shared the first part of Simon's story. We met him again in Chapter

Six to discover his values and again in Chapter Seven regarding people pleasing and boundaries. I wonder if you're curious to find out how things turned out for him.

Simon's Story Part Two

Simon's first session with me was a turning point. As he sat across from me, his carefully composed exterior began to crack. For the first time in years, he allowed himself to be vulnerable, sharing the deep sense of disconnection he felt from his own life.

Over the next few months, we began to unravel the layers of expectations and suppressed desires that had controlled his life. Simon started to recognize how he had continually sacrificed his true self to meet everyone else's expectations. He also began to challenge his own internal narratives about success. He realized that his previous definition of achievement—based on corporate ladder climbing—was fundamentally misaligned with his true self.

After eliciting his values in relation to work (discussed in Chapter Six), Simon started making small but significant changes. He began taking evening art classes to fill his need for creativity. At first, he was hesitant, worried about what his colleagues and family might think. But with each class, he discovered a part of himself that had been dormant for decades. His love of art became the focal point of his journey.

His migraines began to subside as he started living more authentically. Simon learned to recognize the difference between genuine connections with people and using people-pleasing behavior to try and gain approval. He practiced setting boundaries and using assertive communication. At work, instead of automatically saying "Yes" to every request, he began to evaluate opportunities based on his values and personal capacity. He said "No" to the offer of a new project that required excessive overtime. There were instances where he slipped back into old people-pleasing patterns, but each time, he became more skilled at recognizing these moments and redirecting himself.

Simon had a difficult conversation with Jazmin, revealing his long-suppressed feelings of dissatisfaction and his desire to explore a different career path that supported his top 5 values (respect, creativity, validation, fun, and financial security). To his surprise, Jazmin was supportive. She had sensed his unhappiness for years but hadn't known how to approach the subject.

In his family life, he became more intentional about setting boundaries. He had a vulnerable conversation with his parents about his childhood, explaining how their expectations had prevented him from pursuing his true passions. While difficult, this conversation opened up a more authentic relationship. His father, surprisingly, talked about his own suppressed dreams and regrets, creating a deeper understanding between them.

Simon also began to explore diversity and challenge the narrow social expectations he had previously accepted. He joined a local art collective that brought together artists from various backgrounds, ages, and life experiences. This exposed him to perspectives he had never considered before. He learned to appreciate different ways of thinking and being, moving away from the rigid corporate mindset that had previously defined his world.

The biggest transformation came when Simon decided to move from his corporate job into something more aligned with his values. He started freelancing as a graphic designer, which combined his business acumen with his creative passion.

It wasn't an easy journey. There were financial challenges, moments of self-doubt, and some difficult conversations with family and friends who were used to the old Simon. But for the first time in his life, he was making choices based on his own desires, not external expectations.

His relationship with Jazmin deepened as he became more authentic. She fell in love with this more vulnerable, passionate version of Simon—a man who was finally true to himself. They developed a new communication style based on honesty and mutual respect, and Simon learned to express his needs and feelings directly. Financial decisions became a collaborative process aligned with their shared values. Instead of working solely to maintain a certain social image, they began making choices that reflected their true priorities— experiences over possessions, personal growth over social status. His children now had a father who encouraged them to follow their dreams, to listen to their inner voice, and to value their own happiness above external validation.

The migraines disappeared completely. The constant feeling of emptiness was replaced by a sense of purpose and excitement about life.

Simon had learned that the most important approval comes from within, and that living life being true to yourself is the greatest form of success.

A Personal Invitation

This isn't the end of your journey—it's the beginning. Your authentic life is a masterpiece in progress, painted with bold strokes of courage, self-love, and unwavering truth. Living authentically means bringing your whole true self to everything you do. It's about being the same person inside and outside, which means your actions match your words, and your words match your beliefs. Being the "real you" all the time might not always be easy, but it's always worth it. What matters is your commitment to showing up again and again for yourself with an open heart and a compassionate spirit.

I invite you to use COMPASS to navigate your way home to you!

You've got this!

Please join our community on Facebook and share your story of transformation (Facebook page: It's Time To Be Me)

https://www.facebook.com/share/4bx2vEqwV5A7U y5h/?mibextid=LQQJ4d

About the Author

Carolyn G.A Ching is the expert other professionals go to study with and the therapist other therapists go to for personal sessions. In addition to her twenty-plus years of private practice in Hawaii and Australia, she also worked with celebrities at the Golden Door health retreat in Australia.

Carolyn divides her time between the beautiful Big Island of Hawaii, where she loves spending time by the ocean, and the Sunshine Coast of Australia, where she has fun with her grandson.

Do you want Carolyn G.A Ching to be the motivational speaker at your next event?

Then email carolyn@absoluteawareness.com.au. Or contact her via her websites www.bigislandhypnosis.com

www.absoluteawareness.com.au

Please join our community on Facebook and share your story of transformation.

(Facebook page: It's Time To Be Me)

https://www.facebook.com/share/4bx2vEqwV5 A7Uy5h/?mibextid=LQQJ4d